UNIVERSITY OF NORTH CAROLINA
STUDIES IN THE ROMANCE LANGUAGES AND LITERATURES
Number 61

STUDIES ON THE
CANCIONERO DE BAENA

STUDIES ON THE
CANCIONERO DE BAENA

BY

CHARLES F. FRAKER, JR.

CHAPEL HILL
THE UNIVERSITY OF NORTH CAROLINA PRESS

depósito legal: v. 451 - 1966.

artes gráficas soler, s. a. — valencia — 1966

CONTENTS

	Pages
CHAPTER I—Judaism in the *Cancionero de Baena*	9
Jewish Polemic	11
Some Doctrinal Currents in Mediaeval Spanish Judaism	20
Skeptic and Scoffer	23
"Sincerity" of the 'Converso' Poets	30
Fernán Sánchez Calavera: Rationalism	34
Calavera: Faith and Doubt	39
A Christian Rabbi?	52
The 'Conversos' in the 'Cancionero de Baena'	59
CHAPTER II—"La poesía es una graçia infusa del señor Dios"	63
CHAPTER III—Astrology in the *Cancionero de Baena*	91
Fortune and Astrology	94
Dante and Astrology	99
Astrology: Nature and Accident	103
The Views of the Clerics	106
A Frustrated Debate on Astrology?	115
CHAPTER IV—The Religious Ideas of Fernán Manuel de Lando	117

Chapter I

JUDAISM IN THE *CANCIONERO DE BAENA*

As is well known, a great many of the poems of the *Cancionero de Baena* date from the early years of the fifteenth century. These were also years that witnessed one of the most remarkable series of events in late mediaeval Spanish history, the conversion of great numbers of Spanish Jews to Christianity. The year 1391 saw in Spain a succession of appalling massacres of Jews throughout the Peninsula, a disaster that came close to destroying completely the Jewish community there. The conversions were the immediate consequence of this occurrence, of course, a much less simple consequence, be it noted, than one might like to imagine.[1] Now, one could hardly expect this exceedingly important moment in Spanish history to go totally unnoticed by the courtier poets of the *Baena* collection. Indeed, the frequent references to Jews and things Jewish has been noticed by critics and historians. It is also not unknown that some of these poets were themselves of Jewish blood.[2] This fact is especially interesting, incidentally,

---

[1] Cf. A. Domínguez Ortiz, *La clase social de los conversos en la edad moderna* (Madrid, 1955), p. 10.

[2] For the possible Jewish origin of Fernán Manuel de Lando see the review by F. Márquez Villanueva in the *Anales de la Universidad Hispalense* of the work of Domínguez Ortiz cited above. J. B. Avalle Arce discusses Baena's Jewish background in "Sobre Juan Alfonso de Baena", *RFH*, VIII, 141 ff.: Avalle does not exclude the possibility that Baena was a *morisco*. Lando and Baena seem to be exchanging insults concerning their new condition as Christians in numbers 370 and 371 in the *Cancionero* [*El Cancionero de Juan Alfonso de Baena*, ed. P. J. Pidal (Buenos Aires, 1949); henceforth I shall refer to poems in the *Baena* collection with Pidal's numbers as CB 370, CB 371, &c.]. The Franciscan Fray Diego de Valencia seems to be on

if we consider that not a few of them were productive in the first ten or fifteen years of the century; this means that their memories of their years before baptism must have been still fresh — in this sense they were strikingly unlike other *conversos* of a later time or generation, who, in fact, had little or no recollection of Jewish life.

What has not been attempted by scholars is an investigation of the poems of the *Cancionero* for traces of the influence of the Jewish religion, properly speaking, or of habits of mind engendered by the Judaism of the poets' time.[3] The study which follows is such an attempt. It must be admitted that, superficially at least, Judaism is a peripheral subject of interest for this generation of poets. Even as they discourse in their candid way about religious and dogmatic matters, other subjects seem to interest them more. However, the discovery of any trace whatever of concern for Judaism perforce tells us a great deal about the intellectual personalities of the poets and indeed markedly colors their remarks on other matters. For example, in a group of poets as deeply fascinated by religious questions as was this, the fact that one or another of the group is a baptized Christian of only a few years' standing, occasionally revealing attitudes and prejudices inherited from his old religion, cannot fail to be significant. It is with this intent of presenting a more complete picture of the intellectual and religious profiles of some of the *Baena* poets that we have seen fit to carry out this investigation.

---

friendly terms with a number of practicing Jews, and also appears to be familiar with the Jewish world generally (CB 501, CB 511). Furthermore one satirical poem of his is generously laced with Hebrew terms of abuse (CB 511). The Judaism of still other poets will be discussed in the course of this chapter.

[3] The presence of Jews or of *conversos* in the list of contributors to the collection, evident from the poems themselves, has been noticed by J. Amador de los Ríos, *Estudios sobre los judíos en España* (Madrid, 1848), pp. 425ff. C. de Puymaigre in *La cour littéraire de don Juan de Castille* (Paris, 1871), p. 131, speaks of "half-converted Jews" as among the authors of the collection. Neither these historians nor Menéndez Pelayo in the *Antología de poetas líricos castellanos* (Madrid, 1947) has anything to say about Judaism, properly speaking.

JEWISH POLEMIC

A poet in the *Baena* collection who is almost certainly of Jewish blood, Fernán Manuel de Lando, has left us an interesting question in verse on a theological theme addressed to a learned Dominican, also author of poems in *Baena*. In this *pregunta* Lando asks the Master of Theology, Fray Alfonso de la Monja, to resolve for him certain difficulties related to the dogmas of the Trinity and the Incarnation:

> En ante qu'el mundo fuese criado,
> Quando eran tinieblas é confusydat,
> Sy era Dios bivo ya en trenidat,
> Pues que non era el Fijo encarnado.
>
> E sy me dezides que syienpre ayuntado
> Fue tryno el Señor en symple unidat,
> ¿Commo vistió la umanidad,
> Dexando los dos al uno apartado? [4]

Lando is here proposing a dilemma: either God was only one Person up to the time of the Incarnation, or else the second Person of the Trinity must have abandoned the other two when He became man. The question is not original. Although it is impossible to find its immediate source, there is good evidence to show that it belongs to a long tradition of Jewish anti-Christian polemic. Thus, the very difficulty presented here — the Word must abandon the Trinity, if He is to become man — is far from unknown in Jewish polemical literature. Substantially the same question appears in an anonymous fifteenth century polemical poem — a work of Italian origin, possibly — a handbook of stock arguments to be used against Christians. [5] Here the issue is the separation of the Father and the Son:

---

[4] CB 281.

[5] *Memoir of the Nizzachon of Rabbi Lipmann*, tr. O. Rankin in *Jewish Religious Polemic* (Edinburgh, 1956), p. 61. Rankin (p. 51) favors the view that the author of this piece is Messhulam ben Uri of Modena.

How were the Father and the Son then separated [at the Incarnation, of course],
When according to their opponents' [i.e., our opponents', the Christians'] own words the
Father and the Son were united
Up to the time of the second Temple in its finished state?

Since it is very unlikely that the anonymous author copied from Lando, the virtual identity of the arguments suggests that matter of this sort was generally current in the Jewish community in Europe. What we know of Jewish polemic in the Middle Ages confirms this possibility: apologetic works of widely different origins are often found to contain much the same arguments.

Lando is just the sort of person we would expect to be acquainted with Jewish polemic, and it is not surprising to find echoes of this in his verses. He probably had at one time been a Jew, and his change of religion might well have left him with certain perplexities concerning his new faith. Moreover, Lando's own time, a period of clamorous conversions, was also one of copious and vehement polemic in both camps. The Christians were as desirous as ever to convert the Jews, and the Jews were making every effort to keep or regain their own.[6] The latter concern is the point of the Jewish polemic: not to convert Christians, but to dissuade Jews from turning Christian — or to regain them, if they had been baptized. Jews and Judeo-Christians alike lived in an atmosphere heavily charged with controversy, and it would have been remarkable had Lando not somehow been affected.

Lando's question has all the earmarks of being polemical in character. It is typical of Jewish apologetic on one score above all: it raises difficulties for the dogmas of the Trinity and the Incarnation. Not only are these the two central doctrines of Christianity, they are also the two Christian teachings most hateful to the Jews, zealous as they are in affirming the unity and

---

[6] The Jewish polemic works are those mentioned in this chapter. Christian polemic works of this time include the *Scrutinium Scripturarum* of Pablo de Santa María, the *Hebraeomastix* of Jerónimo de Santa Fe, both mentioned in Domínguez Ortiz, *op. cit.*, p. 16. The passage mentions the effort to convert the Jews.

incorporeity of God. "Be not like thy fathers," says with deep bitterness Profiat Duran, a rabbi of Lando's own time, in a famous letter to an ex-Jew:

> Be not like thy fathers who believe in only one God, from Whom they removed all plurality... who conceived God as immutable, withdrawing Him from any incarnation, seeing in Him nothing but pure spirit. [7]

There hardly exists a Jewish polemic document in which the attack on these two dogmas does not play a large part. The four poems in the *Baena* collection which can in any way be connected to Jewish polemic bear out this truth fully: they all touch on the two mysteries. [8] Anti-Christian polemic does so in general, but more than ever in Lando's own time. It has been pointed out that Hasday Crescas, the great Jewish theologian and philosopher of a few years before, produced in his own polemic treatise a decisive document in this respect. [9] Whereas earlier anti-

---

[7] *Letter to an Apostate,* by Profiat Duran, in E. Fleg, *Anthologie juive,* 6th edition (Paris), II, 123. It will be noticed that Duran's argument that the Incarnation implies a change in Divinity is substantially that of Lando and of the author of the *Memoir.*

[8] The other three will be discussed in the course of this chapter. Incidentally, the first two octaves of one of the three, a piece by Calavera, CB 526, obviously move in the same circle of ideas we have been discussing. His arguments are like Lando's, like those of the *Memoir* and of Duran's letter.

> Maestro señor, quiero vos preguntar,
> Pues es indivisa la Trenidat,
> En commo pudo el Fijo encarnar
> E tomar él en sy la umanidat;
> Ser engendrado el engendrador,
> Salir d'ellos amos el consolador,
> Todos tres eguales non mayor nin menor,
> En una sustançia ssyn se apartar.
>
> E sy d'esta santa é pura asunpçion
> Tomó cada uno d'ellos de parte,
> E ssy d'esto non, commo la union
> De tres se allega é se departe; &c.

[9] I. LOEB, "La controverse réligieuse entre les chrétiens et les juifs au moyen âge en France et en Espagne", *Revue d'histoire des réligions,* XVIII, 148.

Christian matter tended to diffuse its energies over a wide field, dealing, for example, with hundreds of Biblical *loci*, Crescas sets a new fashion by concentrating on what he considers the main doctrines of Christianity which separate it from Judaism. Chief of these, of course, are the Trinity and the Incarnation. This new concentration becomes the rule in fifteenth century polemic matter. Thus, for example, at no less important an occasion than the dispute between Christians and Jews •at Tortosa, the Jewish apologists, impatient with attempts on the Christian side to steer the discussion on to the problem of whether or not the Messiah had been born — a question *they did not deem crucial,* be it noted — requested at one point that the talk turn to more fundamental matters, that of the Trinity and the Incarnation. The words attributed to the rabbis in the records of the dispute express the new emphasis dramatically, in an interesting argument:

> Non est dubium quod illa repugnancia que est in eo propter quod pars quecumque negans secundum legem suam esset heretica censenda si oppositum assereret est valde maior quam illa repugnancia que est in eo cuius si aliqua parcium oppositum crederet non censeretur heretica. Ideo repugnancia que est inter judeum et christianum in incarnacione et trinitate est in eo quod quecumque parcium negans heretica censeretur iuxta fidem eorundem si oppositum assereret. Controversia vero vel repugnancia que est inter eos an messias venerit aut venturus extat est in eo cuius si judeus crederet oppositum non esset hereticam... per consequens sequitur repugnanciam que est inter judeum et christianum in trinitate et in incarnacione maiorem fore quam illa scilicet an iam venerit aut sit venturus messias. [10]

Instances of this sort in Jewish apologetic of this time can be multiplied; Lando's choice of questions conforms to a very general rule.

Lando limits his Jewish polemic to eight lines of verse and a single question. Fernán Sánchez Calavera, on the other hand, in a *pregunta* of *his* which includes Jewish controversial matter,

---

[10] Quoted in F. BAER, "Die Disputation von Tortosa", in *Spanische Forschungen der Görresgesellschaft* (Berlin, 1929), note on p. 317.

fills up several octaves with as many as five questions. The first two of these are, naturally enough, on the Trinity and the Incarnation. These are followed, however, by three other topics taken from Jewish apologetic, difficulties urged against the possibility of the God-man suffering and undergoing humiliation. The first of these three questions deals with a special consequence of the Fall of man: if the salvation of man is the work of the whole Trinity, why was this Mystery hidden from men for so long? Why indeed was salvation so long delayed?

>...ssy Dios trino en todo lugar
>Deviera esta obra por sy acabar,
>E Fijo, Spiritu Santo, deviera escusar
>O salvar el mundo á menos d'esta arte.
>
>E ssu eterna, infynita, eterrnal
>Por qué á los primeros non fué rrevelada,
>E la salvaçion del linaje humanal
>Por qué non fué luego[,] mas tanto alongada: [11]

One odious consequence for the Jew of the Christian doctrine of Original Sin was the notion that the Patriarchs, at death, were not worthy of Heaven and had to wait in Hell for their rescue by Christ. Jewish polemic likes to harp on this supposed injustice. Duran's letter, above mentioned, deals with the subject. So also does the treatise addressed to Pablo de Santa María by his fellow rabbi Josua Halorki on the occasion of Pablo's epoch-making conversion. The Christian apologist of the century before, Alfonso de Valladolid, deals explicitly with the idea as a classic Jewish stumbling block.[12] It is this consequence, of course, that is virtually, at least, on Calavera's mind. But what is to be noted particularly is the fact that Calavera's *formulation* of this question is practically the same as that of a number of Jewish authors.

---

[11] CB 526.
[12] *Die apologetische Schrift des Josua haLorki an der Abtrünnung des Salomon haLewi*, ed. L. Landau (Antwerp, 1906), p. 42. I. Loeb, *op. cit.*, p. 149, discusses the question of whether Josua is one and the same person as Jerónimo de Santa Fe. For A. de Valladolid, see I. Loeb, "Polémistes chrétiens et juifs en France et en Espagne", *Revue des études juifs*, XVIII, 52-63. O. Rankin, *op. cit.*, p. 54, speaks of the attitude of Jews towards the doctrine of the Limbo of the Just.

Calavera asks why Salvation did not come at the beginning. Duran asks why man was left so long in the bondage of Satan.[13] An old French work of polemic traditionally called the *Old Nizzachon* also asks why the era of Grace came so late in history. The anonymous Italian polemical poem above quoted has a passage which asks:

> "Why is his chariot so long in coming" [Judges 5:28] to
> deliver them who put their trust in him?
> And why are the steps of his course so slow
> When he has already paid for his brethren the redemption
> price?[14]

The diversity of our witnesses is striking. It is one more indication that some of our polemical arguments circulated widely.

The rest of the questions asked by Calavera repeat in abbreviated form some of the other stock objections urged against Christianity by Jews:

> E por qué [que] Adam pecó é fallesçió,
> Por qué su linage por él meresçió
> De yr al infierno á do padesçió
> Tormentos crueles é pena cuytada.
>
> E por qué Adan la gloria perdiese
> Por su culpa é fuese á infierno levado,
> Qué meresçió Dios por que assy fuesse
> Por él tan vilmente muy cruçificado;
> De mas que paresçe por muy imposible
> Que Dios padesçiesse sseyendo inpasible,
> O sy solo un omme que fuera pasible [posible?]
> Cunpliera para esto de ser enbiado.

The point in the question on Original Sin is that for Judaism Adam's bequest to his descendants consists only in physical death and the necessity of "eating bread in the sweat of one's brow"; there is no question of inherited guilt and none of abandonment to Hell on account of his sin. Halorki asks in his letter:

---

[13] Duran in Fleg, II, 123.
[14] In O. Rankin, *op. cit.*, p. 62.

> Was not Adam punished enough for his transgression in that he was driven from the Garden of Eden, and that the ground was cursed for his sake, and that he must enjoy its yield only through hardship, bitter labor, and with the sweat of his brow? [15]

Jewish apologists and Calavera with them underline heavily the apparent injustice in the idea of one man undergoing punishment for another's sin. The same objection is extended to the Redemption. These arguments are very easy to find in Hebrew literature; hardly any Jewish apologist omits them. In or immediately before Calavera's time they appear in the polemic writings of Crescas, Duran, Halorki and others. [16]

Also omnipresent in anti-Christian literature is the assertion that the notion is absurd that God should live as a human being, be humiliated, suffer and die. Almost any of the authors we have cited and others as well give us examples of this, Nachmanides, [17] Halorki, Hayyim ibn Musa, Duran. [18] Nachmanides in his own account of the Dispute of Barcelona tells us of this challenge he hurled at his Christian opponents:

> That the Creator of heaven and earth and all that is in them should withdraw into and pass through the womb of a certain Jewess and should grow there for seven months and be born a small child, and after this grow up to be handed over to his enemies who condemn him to death and kill him, after which, you say, he came to life and returned to his former abode—neither the mind of a Jew nor of any man will sustain this.

Also in the same mood of Calavera's question is the problem put by Josua Halorki of how the Origin of matter can Himself be made of matter. This is not an isolated instance. The whole life and mode of being of Christ is subject to attack in a great part of this literature in much these terms. If Christ is indeed God, how can He, as God, suffer thirst, experience fear, or

---

[15] Halorki, *op. cit.*, p. 42.
[16] For Crescas, see note 9; for Duran, Fleg, II, 123; Halorki, p. 42.
[17] "Disputation of Rabbi Moses ben Nachman with Fra Paulo Christiani, 1236", in Rankin, p. 191.
[18] For Crescas, see note 9; for Duran, Fleg II, 123; Hayyim, I. Loeb, "La controverse", pp. 51-52.

undergo death? To the Jewish apologists none of these possibilities seem to square with the divinity Christians claim for Jesus.

Calavera, then, raises some of the classic difficulties put to Christians down the years by Jewish apologists. The obvious Jewish ancestry in particular of the question about the Limbo of the Just by itself persuades us of the polemical nature of the *pregunta*. But what is most convincingly Jewish about this poem is precisely the *selection* of problems raised. A registry of several important Jewish works of polemic shows that Calavera chose some of the very commonest topics of controversy. Thus, his poem deals with the following matters: the Trinity, the Incarnation, Original Sin, the Limbo of the Just, the Redemption, Christ's suffering. In the following list, I include contents of a few Jewish documents. All of them except one are from Lando's time or shortly before; this one, the work by Moses ben Nachman, is about a hundred years earlier, and is perhaps the more interesting on that account:

> Crescas: the Trinity, the Incarnation, the Redemption, Original Sin, the Immaculate Conception, the Eucharist, Baptism, the abandonment of the Law by Christians, the fall of the angels.
>
> Josua Halorki: the Trinity, the Incarnation, Original Sin, the Limbo of the Just, the perpetual virginity of Mary, difficulties related to the notion of the Humanity of Christ, the abandonment of the Law, and a whole series of difficulties for the Messiahship of Christ.
>
> ben Nachman: the Trinity, the Incarnation, the sufferings of Christ, the Christian conception of faith, the Messiahship of Christ, and answers to some of the stock arguments of Christian polemic.
>
> Duran: the Trinity, the Incarnation, the Eucharist, the suffering and death of Christ, Original Sin, the delay of the Redemption, the abandonment of the Law, and an unflattering reference to the Great Schism.
>
> Joseph Albó: the Trinity, the Incarnation, the Eucharist, the abandonment of the Law, comparison of Old and New Testaments. [19]

---

[19] The Albó polemic is found in his work *Ikkarim*, Bk. III, Chap. 25 [trans. I. Husik (Philadelphia, 1930), III, 224ff.]. This is his account of his own arguments against Jerónimo de Santa Fe at the Dispute of Tortosa. He was one of the two rabbis present who did not accept baptism.

Thus, not only the actual matter discussed by Calavera, but in a sense the architecture of his poem convinces us that we are dealing with a sort of miniature polemic treatise. It might be added that Calavera concludes by asserting his faith as a Christian, and the academic nature of his questions. But the thorny problem of Calavera's attitudes to Judaism and Christianity must be set aside for the moment, to be returned to later.

Before abandoning problems related to polemic in the *Cancionero de Baena*, we would do well to consider for a moment the sort of answers that were elicited by the *preguntas* by our two *conversos*. Calavera's piece is addressed to Fray Diego de Valencia, and his answer tells us a good deal about the mood in which polemic was conducted. Here, for example, are his lines on the suffering and death of Christ (against Calavera who wondered how Christ, being God, could suffer and die):

> E vos non creades que Dios padesçiese
> Por culpa de Adan que fué engañado,
> Nin devemos creer inmortal que muriese,
> Ca contra natura es esto provado;
> Mas murió el omme que era visible
> Por culpa del omme que fué enpeçible,
> E non solo omme, sy non Dios unible
> Que salvar pidiese el omme cuytado. [pudiese?] [20]

The point is that the explanation is the obvious one: any student of the catechism is able to state that Christ had two natures, and that it was His human nature that was subject to suffering and death, and not His divine nature. That Calavera should require such a simple answer points up once again his naïveté in things Christian. More important, perhaps, the exchange is entirely symptomatic of the way religious polemic was carried on between Christians and Jews at this time and in the Middle Ages in general. There seemed to be little attempt on either side to understand the real basis of the dogmas of the other. It seems unbelievable to us nowadays that Spanish rabbis, men of such vast culture, at home with Aristotle and his commentators, could really believe that Christianity taught that God *qua* God had a

---

[20] CB 527.

body, or that He was susceptible to passions, or that Christ's glorified Body had to pass physically through all the spheres to get from heaven to the altar where Mass was being celebrated. It seems odd beyond measure that Christians could have imagined that Jews could be impressed with arguments for the Messiahship of Christ, based on texts in the Talmud.[21] Such was the case, however; simple answers like that of Fray Diego would often have been highly useful.

SOME DOCTRINAL CURRENTS IN MEDIAEVAL SPANISH JUDAISM

At this point in our study we must make a parenthesis. Before we go on, it is important that we set forth in a general way some of the doctrinal positions typical of mediaeval Spanish Judaism. It is hardly possible for us to understand the sort of problem our *converso* poets were concerned with, unless we have a fair grasp of what sort of ideas were familiar to them as Jews. I have taken the liberty, therefore, of repeating a few well-known facts — matter available in any handbook — which will permit us to orient ourselves with respect to our poets' old religion. A little arbitrarily, perhaps, we will limit ourselves to two great Jewish doctrinal currents, Philosophy and Cabala. There was undoubtedly a great deal more matter abroad, and all sorts of shadings, but these positions seem fundamental, and they are the ones which shed the most light on our poets and their opinions.

Philosophy,[22] the more intellectual and aristocratic of the two persuasions, could hastily be characterized as allegiance to Aristotle Arabized. It taught that God was Self-knowing Intellect, the First Cause, and unmoved Mover. Ranged below Him were a series of Intelligences, or emanations, each of which, with the

---

[21] The argument that the glorified body of Christ must pass through the spheres is Albó's. See note 19. For Messiahship, see below.

[22] These general remarks about Jewish philosophy apply in full strength to philosophers from Abraham ibn David until Crescas and Albó. A perfectly adequate account of this matter can be found in I. Husik, *A History of Mediaeval Jewish Philosophy* (New York, 1940). The best account of the Cabalism I am describing may be found in G. Scholem, *Major Trends in Jewish Mysticism* (New York, 1941), Chapters V and VI, pp. 156-286.

exception of the last, directly caused the motion of one of the spheres. The lowest of these intelligences, the Active Intellect, was at once the ruler of the sublunar, natural world, and the single light illuminating human minds. It was also the source of Prophecy. It was these doctrines and a few others that formed the common stock of nearly all mediaeval Jewish philosophy for several centuries. [23] Now the relationship of this system of thought to Jewish religion is various and complex. On one hand, there were those that taught the substantial coincidence between the teachings of philosophy and those of revealed religion. Such were Maimonides and Gersonides, for example. Others, on the other hand, took a position not unlike that of the Latin Averroists, asserting that philosophical truth might differ widely from revealed truth, but that men were somehow bound to assent to both. [24] This division of minds is further complicated by the fact

---

[23] Christian scholasticism in general held positions not unlike these. Most mediaeval Christian thinkers (excluding the so-called Averroists) departed from them in a number of ways, however. Their ideas about God were rather more complex in the sense that they thought of Him as a Trinity of Persons. They multiplied considerably the number of angels beyond those required to move the spheres. They conceived of not one but many Active Intellects, each a part of the individual human soul. It follows from this, of course, that they thought about the management of the sublunar world in a different way. Finally, they held widely different views on the relationship of reason and revelation. Few, if any, Christians held that the contents of revelation was identical to the things discoverable by reason. For the Christian schoolman there may have been single revealed doctrines that reason could confirm, but the whole range of *revelata* contained much beyond the scope of reason. [Cf. E. Gilson, *Reason and Revelation in the Middle Ages* (New York, 1958)]. The opposite is the stated position of Gersonides, for example (see below note 48). Much the same can be said of Maimonides, a virtual adherent to what H. Wolfson calls a "single faith theory of rationalist type" [see Wolfson, *Double Faith Theory in Clement of Alexandria, Saadia, Averroes and St. Thomas* (Philadelphia, 1942), p. 243]. Leo Strauss also considers it Maimonides' doctrine that the teachings of reason and the teachings of revelation are identical ["The Literary Character of the *Guide of the Perplexed*" in *Essays on Maimonides*, ed. S. Baron (New York, 1941), p. 44]. On the identification of the two teachings in mediaeval Jewish philosophy see J. Guttmann, *Die Philosophie des Judentums* (Munich, 1933), pp. 71ff. It should be added, incidentally, that there is a strong anti-rationalist strain in Jewish theology which has little to do with Cabala. Judah Halevy belongs to this line. Nachmanides, also an important anti-rationalist, is a moderate Cabalist.

[24] Cf. G. VAJDA, "A propos de l'averroïsme juif", *Sefarad*, XII, 1ff., especially the pages devoted to Isaac Albalag (pp. 21ff.).

that the religiously orthodox Aristotelians often took a very liberal and, as it were, "modernist" view of the meaning of Scripture, and were not at all adverse to enunciating certain doctrines quite at variance with the obvious sense of the Bible. Some, for example, denied that God knew particulars; almost all denied that Providence affected particulars; [25] others had doubts about personal immortality, and so forth. In general, it was easy to accuse all shades of philosophical Jews of religious skepticism; the accusation was often made in the time our poets wrote and earlier. [26] As we shall see, many of the questions they ask on all sorts of subjects grow out of this skeptical and critical mood.

Philosophy's great rival within Judaism in Spain was, of course, Cabala. Unlike philosophy, Cabala, popular, pietist, devotional, represented for many a bulwark of more stringent orthodoxy, a defense against the corroding effects philosophical reasoning had upon belief in revelation. Mythological and poetic rather than rational and discursive, the system of Cabala is complex and hard to summarize. Perhaps its fundamental notion is a doctrine of correspondences, correspondences of things and events on earth with spiritual realities. Not with God simply, however: this would imply for the Cabalist a complexity, a structure in the idea of God quite out of concord with his notion of the En Sof, nameless, absolute, unutterable, a divine Nothing. The correspondence is with the Sephirot, a structured group of reflections or emanations of Divinity, distinct from It, but dependent on It, joined to It "as a flame to the candle-wick" [27] and forming in a sense one thing with It. Everything in the world, all its rich

---

[25] These two propositions, along with the notion that the Agent Intellect is one for all men, were included in the list of propositions condemned by Bishop Tempier at Paris in 1277 [E. Gilson, *Christian Philosophy in the Middle Ages* (New York, 1955), pp. 403, 407, 728]. These condemnations profoundly affected the subsequent history of scholastic philosophy. After this time hardly any Christian writer held the positions we have mentioned except for the Averroists (for the importance of the condemnations of 1277, see Gilson, *op. cit.*, pp. 403ff.). The influence of the Averroists in Spain, by the way, appears to have been slight. Carreras y Artau, *Historia de la filosofía cristiana* (Madrid, 1943) is able to name only one, Tomás Escoto, active in the early fourteenth century (pp. 494ff.).

[26] See below, notes 56 and 60 of this chapter.

[27] The expression is a commonplace in Cabala (see G. Vajda, "La conciliation de la philosophie et de la loi réligieuse", *Sefarad*, X, 30).

variety, its mixture of good and evil, is prefigured in the Sephirot. By the same token, the inner structure and activity of the Sephirot are symbolized and represented by things on earth. Perhaps the dominant note in Cabala is just this sense of the nearness of God, and of His accessibility through the Sephirot, of the possibility it promises the Jew of entering an intimate and cordial relationship with Him.

All this is far removed from the abstractness and intellectuality of philosophical Judaism, and it is natural that a good deal of hostility should have existed between the two schools. The very curious work in Arabic by Joseph ben Abraham ibn Waqar called, in fact, *The Conciliation of Philosophy with Religious Law* is nothing other than a full-scale attempt to harmonize the two doctrines. Short of this, there were numerous Cabalistic writers who to some degree borrowed notions from philosophy, and though it was less common for philosophers to use Cabalistic matter, such is not unknown.[28]

SKEPTIC AND SCOFFER

We may immediately put these generalizations to work as we study an anonymous poem in the *Baena* collection, a composition which is highly revealing of the world of ideas of Jews and Judeo-Christians in the early fifteenth century. This remarkable piece is a *pregunta* addressed to the poet Gonçalo Martínez de Medina; it is a strange, unsystematic catch-all, including questions on

---

[28] On attempts to harmonize philosophy and Cabala, see G. Vajda, "La conciliation," *Sefarad*, IX, 311-357, X, 26-73, 281-325; and by the same author *Juda ben Nissim ibn Malka, philosophe marroquain* (Paris, 1954), and "Le traité pseudo-Maimonidéen," *Archives d'histoire doctrinale et littéraire du moyen âge*, XX, 83. Spanish Judaism after Crescas, with its rigid and defensive orthodoxy, tended to favor reconciliations of this sort. Zenoch Duran, a disciple of Crescas, incorporates Cabalistic elements into his thought [G. Vajda, *Introduction à la pensée juive* (Paris, 1927), p. 183]. Albó speaks of the Sephirot (v. III, p. 224); Crescas himself uses the concept of Sephirah [H. A. Wolfson, *Crescas' Critique of Aristotle* (Cambridge, Mass., 1929), pp. 459ff.]. One of these poems we shall deal with (CB, end of 340) addresses questions about Cabala to "filosofos". This apparent incongruity is in all likelihood explained by the fact that in these years theologians, Cabalists and philosophers were all the same people.

subjects as unlike as medicine and versification. The classic pair of questions about the Trinity and the Incarnation appear, but the work is not merely a piece of anti-Christian polemic. Certain theological disputes within Judaism are held up to ridicule, making the mood of the piece as much anti-Jewish as anti-Christian. Most unusual of all, we find a strange blending of the two religions, in lines in which the Trinity is discussed in terms of Jewish mysticism.

The tone of the anonymous poem is, of course, mocking and skeptical. No intellectual field that normally invites belief seems valid to the author, whether it calls itself medicine, astrology, philosophy or religion. As regards the last two, the author seems equally contemptuous of three systems, Christianity, Cabala and philosophy. The final pair are, of course, the two schools of thought that divided the Jewish community in Spain, though the poet is hardly persuaded that doctrinal peace reigns even within one camp. Here is his account (in questions) of the internal strife in effect within Judaism:

> A filosofos digo que digan, sy fuera
> Algund sser ante que sser paresçiese,
> E ante que çielos é tierra oviesse
> El señor muy alto en qué grado era:
> Sy en claridat ó en teniebra fiera
> O sy fue el mundo de sienpre fundado,
> O sy paresçió de nuevo criado,
> O sy fué causa alguna primera. [29]

Roughly there are four matters in these few lines, the teachings of the two rival schools, Cabala and Philosophy, and the doctrinal wrangling within each. The unknown poet's attitude towards all this is skeptical. We gather this from the nature of the questions he asks: all are malicious. He is impressed at times with the apparent inner absurdity of some of the doctrines, and at others by the multiplicity of contradictory points of view of rival teachers. The latter is the case in the questions which bear on philosophy. His question on whether or not the world was "de sienpre fun-

---

[29] Last seven strophes of CB 340. A. Castro has remarked on the Jewish ancestry of the expression "criar de nuevo" [*La realidad histórica de España* (México, 1954), p. 572].

dado" was in the later Middle Ages a sore point, so to speak, for Jewish philosophers. Maimonides, as we know, takes the doctrine of the eternity of the world into account and attacks it. Many later writers accept, like him, Creation in time. Other later philosophers of "Averroist" stamp, notably Isaac Albalag, claim that this is too great a concession of reason to revelation and assert the doctrine of the world's eternity, in agreement with Aristotle, Averroes and others. So it is that the poet finds philosophy a house divided on an important subject, one in which an important religious dogma is at stake.[30]

Our anonymous *converso* is not friendly to Cabala either. His query as to whether there was "algund sser ante que sser paresçiese" is a disdainful reference to the Cabalistic concept of God, one which, in its desire to plumb the Absolute, denies Him even the attribute of Being.[31] Being, say some, can indeed be attributed to certain of the Sephirot, but for some schools of Cabala it is absurd to speak of these as existing before the world was generated. Before this moment Divinity was utterly nameless, utterly enveloped in darkness, a divine Non-being, precisely. It is clear that the poet is phrasing his question so as to make the whole doctrine seem ridiculous. He asks, in effect, if it is plausible to say that something was (i. e., God) before such a thing as Being existed. For him the notion stands self-condemned.

The poet's next question moves in much the same territory: before heaven and earth were created, "el señor muy alto en qué grado era". *Grado*, "degree", is a stock synonym in Cabalistic literature for Sephirah. The *claridat* and *teniebra* in the next

---

[30] Maimonides on creation in time: *Guide for the Perplexed*, trans. Friedländer (New York, 1956), II, Chap. 13-26, pp. 171-220; Gersonides on the same subject: *Milhamot Adonai* (Leipzig, 1866), Bk. VI, 1, Chap. 1-13, pp. 293-353, Chap. 15, pp. 356ff. For Albalag, see G. Vajda, "A propos", p. 24. A Catalonian rabbi of strong anti-philosophical bias, Joseph ben Shalom Ashkenazy accused philosophers of teaching the doctrine of the eternity of the world. In common with other Cabalists, he opposed this doctrine vehemently (G. Vajda, "Un chapitre de l'histoire du conflit entre la Kabbale et la philosophie," *Archives d'histoire doctrinale et littéraire du moyen âge*, 1951, p. 58).

[31] "Ser ante ser" is a common doctrine in Cabala (*Zohar*, II, 42-3).

verse are also significant terms: *claridat*, [32] light, can also mean Sephirah, while *teniebra* probably refers to En Sof, God Himself, Who is divine Darkness, or conceivably also to the first Sephirah, who is described by some writers as a hidden Light, or even a dark Light. The drift of the question is this, more or less: it is supposed that some of the Sephirot came into being simultaneously with the world, while in the view of some authors, others of these emanations are eternal. The poet is asking, in effect, which Sephirot fall into which class, that is to say, which were already in existence at the beginning of the world. Again the question is malicious. Opinions on questions of this sort are legion. One author, ibn Waqar, records both the opinion that only the highest Sephirah is eternal and the view that the first triad of Sephirot are eternal. [33] Other authors seem to imply that all the Sephirot at one time came into being. Once more, the poet finds his presumed teachers unable to agree on important matters.

The variety of conflicting opinions in Cabalistic literature is, in fact, astonishing. The difficulty of drawing consistent doctrine from vast, formless, poetico-prophetic works like the *Zohar* should be obvious. But even systematic treatises such as seem to have been produced in the later Middle Ages show a multitude of interpretations in many areas. The matter of the number of Sephirot, for example, is subject to endless discussion. Ten is the standard number. Ibn Waqar, however, in his survey of Cabalistic thought, reports that some held for twenty, others for thirty or thirty-one, some for as many as three hundred and ten. [34] His information is easy to corroborate. Another question which, according to the same authority, preoccupied grave minds was whether the term First Cause was applicable to God Himself, to the first Sephirah, or to the first triad of Sephirot. And so it goes on the widest variety of subjects, the functions of each Sephirah,

---

[32] G. SCHOLEM, *Die jüdische Mystik in ihren Hauptströmen* (Jerusalem, 1941), p. 432, n. 29 to Chap. VI: "Die Ausdrücken 'Stufen' und 'Lichter' worden am haüfigsten für die Sefiroth gebraucht." This note does not appear in the English edition.

[33] G. VAJDA, "La conciliation", *Sefarad*, X, pp. 31-33. Albó (*op. cit.*, III, 224) affirms, for example, that the first triad of Sephirot is eternal.

[34] G. VAJDA, *Ibid.*, pp. 30-31; Scholem, *Major Trends*, p. 213. Joseph ben Shalom holds for thirty Sephirot (Vajda, "Un chapitre," pp. 57-58).

metempsychosis and many others.[35] All this is undoubtedly the real object of our anonymous poet's mockery.

It should be pointed out that he is not the only person to ridicule mediaeval Spanish Judaism for its supposed doctrinal confusion. Alfonso de Valladolid, a converted Jew and one of the most important Christian apologists in Spain, devotes a lengthy passage in one of his polemic works to a catalog of extravagant and contradictory opinions held by his former correligionists.[36] He refers to the belief of some Jews in ten "persons" in God (an obvious Christianized reference to Sephirot). He reports a bewildering variety of beliefs about the after-life and metempsychosis, that unclean animals are reincarnate sinners and Gentiles, that only Jews rise again or that just Gentiles do also, that in the world to come there is no bodily activity, and to the contrary. The origin of the world is variously explained, that it is eternal, and autonomous, that it is eternal, but dependent on God, that it was created in time, that God makes and destroys many worlds. Some Jews, says our apologist, teach that the Messiah is already alive, though not reigning, others that he has not yet been born. This same variety of doctrines, so stressed, and indeed exaggerated by Alfonso de Valladolid, is also reflected, though indirectly, in the fact that Jewish theology in the fifteenth century was given over in large part to the attempt to enunciate the "fundamental doctrines" of Judaism, that is, in effect, to sort out the essential from the non-essential in all this body of matter. This was the great achievement of some of Crescas' pupils, for example. The simplification became a great need for Jews as pressure from the Christian world increased and Jewish unity became imperative.[37]

---

[35] VAJDA, "La conciliation", *Sefarad*, X, 32.

[36] This is in the *Batallas del Señor*, quoted in I. Loeb, "Polémistes", pp. 60-62. As Loeb points out, this passage is incorporated into Fr. Alonso Espina's *Fortalitium fidei*.

[37] On the question of fundamental doctrines see J. Sarachek, *The Doctrine of the Messiah in Mediaeval Jewish Literature* for Crescas' interest in the problem. Vajda ("Introduction", p. 183) discusses Crescas' disciple Zenoch Duran in this connection. Albó is the author most commonly associated with this problem (*Ikkarim*, and I. Husik, *History*, pp. 407ff. which paraphrases the relevant passages in Albó's major work).

Christianity is, of course, no more exempt from our poet's skepticism and contempt than is either brand of Judaism. He shows this by asking the classic questions about the Trinity and the Incarnation: whether there can be multiplicity in unity, how unchanging God can father an earthly child. With regard to the Trinity, however, he adds a query that is worthy of special attention:

> ...qual ha mas grado ó mas cantidat,
> El Padre ó el Fijo ó el Spiritu santo,

"Grado" confronts us once more. Our *converso* is attempting to understand the Trinity in terms of the Sephirot, as though the three sacred *Persons* were ranged like Sephirot in some order of importance. As we saw, this comparison was made elsewhere by Alfonso de Valladolid who refers to the Sephirot as "Persons" by analogy to the Trinity. Incidentally, although Medina, in his answer to the *pregunta,* makes no special reference to the Sephirot, in another work he does indeed take cognizance of the equation Person-Sephirah. He attacks it very explicitly in the following terms:

> La Deydad es un ser infynido,
> Ser, en que es ser de sienpre engendrado,
> E d'estos seeres otro ser benydo
> Es proçediente en un *ygual grado*.

These lines are, of course, about the procession of Persons within the Trinity, the Son, begotten of the Father, the Holy Spirit proceeding from both. It is interesting to note that this poem contains elements which are almost certainly polemical in intent. The object of the attack has little to do with Jewish-Christian controversy: instead, it is a form of extreme predestinarianism, probably of Wyclifite origin. This predestinarianism is well known to the poets of Medina's acquaintance: the conclusion of the poem is an impassioned vindication of free will and of man's ability to win divine favor freely. As we will see presently, other passages in the poem are addressed in a mode of polemic to the Jews. If, then, this poem has a strong flavor of controversy, we might well be led to suspect that the "ygual grado" I have underscored is a

Jewish reference. In polemic terms it would be pointless for Medina to stress the equality of "degree" of the Holy Ghost with the other Persons, unless there were some sort of rival doctrine maintaining the contrary. Since Trinitarian heresies are virtually unknown at this time, and since another detail in the poem which we will consider shortly makes it even more clear that Medina is addressing Jews at this point, we can only conclude that "grado" is an echo of Cabalistic usage. We may guess, then, that the tendency to compare the procession of Persons to the emanation of Sephirot is a general one, and represents a naïve attempt on the part of many newly converted Jews to understand in terms of something familiar what must have been for them an especially baffling doctrine. [38]

A final question regarding our poem: how do we know that the author was a *converso* and not just a skeptical Jew? One indication is the fact that the poet makes, at one point, a casual reference to man's fallen nature. Speaking of the uncertainty of astrological knowledge, he brings to bear the matter of "nuestro juysio caydo" as rendering such a science invalid. The appearance in the poem of this undoubtedly Christian view of the fall of man serves to convince us that he is indeed a convert to Christianity of some sort, that he is not simply an unbaptized Jew. Such indeed would be implausible even if this detail were missing; the fact that he is poetizing in Castilian within a whole set of culturally "Christian" conventions argues against it. It is well, however, that the poet's status as a *converso* be as clearly established as possible, particularly as such has great bearing on our next topic.

We must not abandon this strange *pregunta* without considering for a moment the person to whom it is addressed, Gonçalo Martínez de Medina. What is striking is the fact that the anonymous poet puts to Medina a whole series of questions having to do with Judaism. This can only mean that Medina was known

---

[38] It should be noted that this quasi-Cabalistic discussion of the Trinity antedates by quite a while the most famous attempts to Christianize Cabala (that of Pico della Mirandola, for example); for other early examples of the Christian use of Cabala, see F. Secret, "Les débuts du Kabbalisme chrétien en Espagne," *Sefarad*, XVII, 36ff.

to his questioner to be himself a *converso* and thus at home with
Jewish doctrines. What we know otherwise about Medina confirms
this possibility. He was acquainted with the concept of the Sephirot and, as we shall see, he knew about Jewish polemic in
some detail. The most curious piece of evidence on Medina's
origin, however, is the fact that the anonymous author puts to
Medina questions on the subject of medicine. Medina's answer,
by the way, shows him fairly familiar with medical procedure.
It hardly seems necessary to remind ourselves that medicine was
virtually a Jewish or *converso* monopoly in Medina's time and a
good many years before and after.[39] The exchange of question
and answer is thus highly significant. One may, therefore, safely
include Medina in the group of poets of this time who are probably of Jewish origin.

"SINCERITY" OF THE CONVERSO POETS

A great part of this study is given over to the religious
opinions of what must have been members of the first generation
of *conversos* in Spain. We might well ask at this point what, in
the most general terms, these newly baptized persons thought
of their new religion. If we may put the question without senti-
mentality, we might ask simply how sincere they were. It was
very easy at this time to point out the huge vested interests they
were defending by turning Christian, and conclude that their
Christianity was cynical, feigned, and that they were unbelieving
to the last. The facts are not so simple, however. In a way it
would be hard to find a more paradoxical frame of mind as
touches religion than that of some of the *Baena* poets. Moreover,
there is considerable diversity. It would be unwise to lump together all these men in our minds without making proper distinctions.

In answering our question we will limit our discussion to the
three "theologizing" poets in *Baena* who not only display identifiably Jewish matter in their works, but who at some point in

---

[39] A. Castro, *op. cit.*, pp. 460-471.

their arguments, provisionally at least, take the side of Judaism against Christianity. These are Lando, Calavera and the anonymous author of the *pregunta* to Martínez de Medina. In the case of the last the question of his sincerity is easily answered. He conforms in a way to the common notion of the early *converso*, cynical, skeptical, religiously indifferent, persuaded that Paris was worth a Mass. Domínguez Ortiz, a historian in the main friendly to Judeo-Christians, gives us this topical convert in the following:

> Fue la parte más elevada de la comunidad judía que mostró menos repugnancia al abandono de su antigua fe; esta porción más culta y rica era también en muchos sentidos la más inmoral, la más corrompida y la menos creyente; su lujo insultante y su dureza de corazón no herían menos a sus propios correligionarios que a los cristianos; en cierto modo, su conversión puede considerarse como el desenlace del cisma latente, que venía oponiendo en las aljamas a los palaciegos y enriquecidos de tibia fe frente a los modestos artesanos que mostraron más constancia en las adversidades. [40]

Incidentally this type of obviously insincere convert figures as the author of at least one other poem in *Baena*: Nicolás de Valencia cynically asks if the birth of Christ is not a sanction for adultery, in that God "begot" a Son by someone else's wife:

> Señor, nos savemos que muger casada
> Que tenga marido, maguera cuytado,
> Que biva con él muy desconsolada,
> Sy quier tomar á otro, que fase pecado;
> E yo sobre esto tengo maginado
> Que non fas pecado nin comete error,
> Pues que lo fiso Dios nostro Señor
> Al santo Joseph que era desposado
>
> Con sancta Maria... [41]

That this picture of the *converso* as a false Christian is not the whole story is patent from the vastly more complex examples

---

[40] Domínguez Ortiz, *op. cit.*, pp. 10-11.
[41] CB 485.

of Lando and Calavera. The body of their writings bears witness to their clearly genuine, though not always successful attempts to find a rationale in Christianity. In the case of Lando (whose thought we will discuss at length in a later chapter) [42] we find a man of intelligence, with a real taste for coherence, whose scattered thoughts on religion, taken as a whole, display remarkable harmony and consistency. Though his "system", if we may call it that, shows a distinct rationalist and antisupernaturalist bias (as does philosophical Judaism, to a great extent), still he is at pains to include in it a number of important Christian elements. He confesses the Trinity in a crucial passage. Salvation is an important notion to him. What he considers to be the effects of the redemptive work of Christ is discussed by him in some detail. Often, to be sure, his conclusions are far from orthodox, but there is no evidence whatsoever that this was intentional. His doctrinal vagaries seem rather to be byproducts of his attempt to make some sense out of his new religion, an attempt he makes, after all, with scant formal theological equipment, even with scant familiarity with Christianity. The most that can be said for his taste for heresy is that he seems resolved to "go it alone" theologically, and depend more on his own wit than on formal learning in thinking about religion. But at no point does he seem intent on counterposing some doctrine of his own to that proposed by orthodoxy.

Whatever the complexities of Lando's life and thought, one poem of his in particular seems singularly devoid of the cynicism that is supposed by some to characterize the early *conversos*. That is his *dezir* in praise of St. Vincent Ferrer. [43] In this not unreadable poem, which is so characteristic and so full of Lando's special ideas and interests, he expresses in the most candid terms admiration for the saint, a contemporary of his, whom he may have known. He paints Vincent as a classic Evangelical figure, of great austerity of personal life, teaching all to serve God without reserve, touching hardened sinners, bringing them to do penance, reconciling enemies, and the rest. The poet notes also his solid learning and his skill in explaining

---

[42] See the study on Lando in this volume.
[43] CB 287.

> Las dubdas escuras que son peligrosas
> A los ynorantes en la fé cristiana,

and at demolishing with dialectic belief in black arts and in false notions about the stars. The tone of the poem makes it impossible to believe that this is an empty occasional piece. Everything is candor here surely. For example we find the poet's person intruding on his work in a way that is striking. With some bitterness he contrasts Ferrer with less holy religious he has known:

> Yo vy muçhos ommes de religion,
> Señoras é monjas de alta loança,
> Tratar luengós tienpos con grant afiança
> E non acabar un solo perdon:
> Mas aqueste justo, perfecto varon,
> Syn les rrequerir nin les suplicar,
> Los injuriados le vienen buscar
> E todos perdonan de buen coraçon.

Later in the poem he feels the need to justify himself:

> Non me quieran mal algunos señores,
> Letrados é sabios que son en Castilla,
> Nin ayan nin tengan á grand maravilla
> Por que yo desir d'él tan altos loores:
> Antes rrevoquen sus viles errores
> Los que contra él fueren rretratantes,
> Que muchos comigo estan concordantes,
> Teologos altos é grandes doctores.

The intrusion of the poet into his own work is not an unusual occurrence in this generation of poets. Much of their production is what we might call conversational: their works were either addressed to specific persons, or at any rate were meant to be circulated among few people. Under such circumstances intrusions of this sort are inevitable. We need not on this account dismiss from our minds here the notion of the "integral man" spoken of by Castro, the one for whom "la realidad es la vivida por la persona total, y no la objetivada por la razón". [44] Lando's verses on

---

[44] A. Castro, *op. cit.*, p. 232.

St. Vincent Ferrer do not make up a profound religious poem. They do seem to show however, that the author's admiration for the saint was cordial and total. This in turn would suggest that Lando's Christianity was more than perfunctory.[45]

FERNÁN SÁNCHEZ CALAVERA: RATIONALISM

The question of Calavera's attitude towards Christianity, of its sincerity above all, is a difficult and complex one. Moreover, it is one that forces itself upon us as we study his work. This is much more true of him than it is of Lando, for example. Lando in *his* poems is given to bold and unambiguous statements of doctrine. They are statements his contemporaries may have disagreed with, or thought foolish; they could not have doubted their meaning. Calavera, on the other hand, is very hard to corner. He seems oddly attracted to perplexities and paradoxes. He contradicts himself more than once. He is at his most characteristic, not when he makes statements, but when he asks questions. Little of this is in a spirit of irony or play, be it noted. Everything in Calavera is in deep earnest. Line after line of his seems to draw his readers into the world of his own personal doubts and dilemmas. In a word, Calavera's ambivalent attitude towards Christianity is the single great underlying motive of much of his doctrinal verse. An accurate appraisal of this attitude will therefore have to depend on a fairly detailed familiarity with the way he develops a number of important themes.

One important element in Calavera's thought which gives rise to some of his intellectual dilemmas is unquestionably part of his Jewish heritage. This is his *rationalism*. The passage in which

---

[45] Of course, it must not be imagined that this poem is devoid of commonplaces or of inherited patterns of thought. This is an age of prophetism and of Joachimism, in the broadest sense. St. Vincent, a preacher of the Last Things and the occasion of the conversion of great numbers of Jews, must hav, and indeed did, appealed to what we might call the Joachimite imagination. Lando's interest in him is significant in this regard, and the poet's basic Joachimism comes through in several details, the hostility he shows to professed religious, for example; it is notable that their chief defect in Lando's eyes is their failure in offices of charity.

he gives utterance to this frame of mind is thoroughly and unmistakably Jewish in its outlook. In what is perhaps Calavera's most famous poem, the great *pregunta* on predestination addressed to Pero López de Ayala, there is a passage in which the poet tells us that certain devout religious had advised him not to scrutinize too closely the secrets of God, but rather to believe in deep simplicity the obvious sense of Scripture.[46] To this he objects that wise men have *always* sought out the deep things of God and what He has truly hidden has never been revealed in any form:

> La cura otro ssy tan poco aprovecha
> Que los rreligiossos en mí obraron,
> Que la entençion de Dios mas derecha
> De la ley syenpre los sabios buscaron:
> E los secretos de Dios que vedaron
> A vos de ssaber en la su estoria,
> Son los que él tiene en la su memoria,
> Que nunca en escripto jamas se fallaron.

To see the drift of these rather obscure lines we must have some fairly clear notion of the relation of philosophy to revelation in rationalist, philosophical Judaism, particularly of its idea of the meanings of Scripture in relation to philosophic truth. To begin with, this is an unfamiliar relation to students acquainted with mediaeval Christian thought. The intellectual world of Maimonides and of other Jewish thinkers of this general type was not the two-storied world of the Christian scholastics, who set

---

[46] The *pregunta* in question is CB 517. The arguments the monks use, incidentally, lead one to believe that Calavera is referring to Hieronymites. The text seems, for example, to make the monks speak of the Bible as the one rule of faith. This is in consonance with Hieronymite "Biblicism" which A. Castro draws attention to in "Lo hispánico y el erasmismo", *RFH*, IV, 15. Furthermore, Calavera's monks urge him to abandon his questions and practice naked faith. It is apparently an important part of the Hieronymite outlook to value Christian practice above knowledge and speculation. This theme is stressed in what appears to be a manual for Hieronymite monks or novices [described in F. Márquez Villanueva, *Investigaciones sobre Juan Alvarez Gato* (Madrid, 1960)], and in the works of two poets closely associated with the Hieronymites, Ayala (CB 518) and Gato (Foulché Delbosc, *Cancionero castellano del siglo XV*, I, no. 124). Needless to say, these aspects, as well as others, of the Hieronymite spirituality deserve a vastly more detailed study than we are able to give it in one brief footnote.

limits to reason in exploring the things of God and left a residue, so to speak, of revealed truth not in conflict with reason, to be sure, but incapable of being established or confirmed by her. Jewish thought tended rather to say that the domains of reason and revelation were coextensive, that Scripture and tradition expressed things one way, and that philosophy expressed much the same things another. The prophets, the sacred authors, wrote in allegories and obscure metaphors, says Maimonides in effect, and it remained for philosophers to declare unequivocally the true meanings of these.[47] To be sure, the weak and the simple do well to remain in their thinking within the obvious and literal sense of these fictions, lest they sin or become unfaithful. But on the other hand, unquestionably, philosophy is the nobler way, and is, in fact, the very perfection of human life.

If, then, reason and revelation really have the same subject matter, it follows that the paths that the mind builds between the two must be two-way streets. On one hand, as Gersonides says, whatever is discovered by reason must be found in the Law, even if this entails its rather subtle interpretation, and, on the other, whatever revelation proposes as true must be susceptible to explanation by philosophic reasoning.[48] We see then on one hand why Maimonides is at such pains to try to reconcile God's incorporeity with passages in the Bible which speak of Him as having a body, and on the other why he and other philosophers devote lengthy chapters to Prophecy, for example, or to miracles, or to the rationale of certain precepts of the Law. It is this latter principle, by the way, — that philosophy should be able to explain revelation — that renders Jews unable to make any sense of the dogma of the Trinity. How can anything be revealed that is "against reason"? Entirely typical is the following passage from Joseph Albó, in which he attacks the notion that this mystery is contained in figures in the Old Testament:

---

[47] *Guide*, II, 29-32, pp. 204-220, II, 47-48, pp. 247-250. See also above, note 23. It should again be stressed that there were also important non-rationalists among mediaeval Jewish thinkers. Calavera's ideas reflect one particular — though at his time and in his class, very important — current in Jewish thought.

[48] Levi ben Gerson, *Milhamot*, VI, II, Chap. 1, p. 419 (note in Husik, *History*, which paraphrases this passage on p. 357).

> The Torah says nothing about the Trinity because it is not true from the point of view of reason, and the Torah does not inculcate an idea that is not true, such as that one is three and three are one while remaining separate and distinct, as they say. The statement of the philosophers that God is Intellect, intelligent and intelligible, and at the same time One is a different thing. For they do not believe that there are in Him three different things, self-existing, Heaven forbid... But that there should be in Him three distinct things, each one existing by itself and that they should nevertheless be one, this is impossible, unless two contradictories can be true at the same time, which is opposed to the primary axioms, and inconceivable by the mind. [49]

Profit Duran expresses the same "philosophical" bias in much cruder and simpler terms. In his violently bitter letter to his baptized Jewish friend he says sarcastically:

> Refrain carefully from putting any value on the first figure of the syllogism: it will oblige you to deny your faith, for you must say: the Father is God, God is the Son, therefore the Father is the Son.

Ben Nachman, a moderate Cabalist, has the same attitude towards the doctrine of the Trinity; he stresses that no one can believe what he cannot understand. [50]

---

[49] Albó, op. cit., III, 224.
[50] Duran, Fleg, II, 123; ben Nachman, in Rankin, op. cit., p. 210. Incidentally, the first lines of Gonçalo Martínez de Medina's long poem (CB 337), the ones which sustain the comparison between the Sephirot and the Persons of the Trinity, are also an attack on the rationalist analysis of the content of revelation. If we are convinced that this passage is addressed to Jews, what other drift could we see in these lines?

> ...todos [the Three Persons] consysten un ser inflamado
> De inflamaçion de grand permanençia,
> *Que por juysio nin inteligençia*
> *Es muy inposible de se conpesado.*
> ...E commo sea myrable é escura
> La interpretaçion del misterio sancto
> E fecho tan alto, que memorya inpura
> Non es abondable á conprehender tanto;
> E todos los sabios rreçiben espanto,
> Por ende, yo tomo la fe por escudo, &c.

Calavera, then, sides with Albó in affirming the sufficiency of reason in regard to the things of God. He misses the point of the advice given him by the Hieronymites. Without oversimplifying their position too much it is probably safe to say that in urging him to accept with simple faith the plain sense of Scripture, they were not attempting to shut off argument. What they were saying was that the Bible in its obvious meaning at bottom tells us as much concerning predestination as can be known. To go further is vain curiosity. Predestination is a mystery essentially, we might say ontologically. The plain sense of Scripture, far from veiling the matter in obscure language, perhaps actually brings us as close to this mystery as our minds can come. Their stand is thus the exact opposite of the Jewish rationalist one. The Bible for them does not speak obscurely about clear matters, but rather speaks as clearly as possible about essentially obscure matters.

Calavera fails to understand all this because at heart he is persuaded that the opposite is true, that the Prophets set down in metaphor truths explainable in more rational terms. This is evidently the point of this remark that the only secrets of God utterly unavailable to us are those which were never included in Scripture. If we combine this notion on these matters with the prestige philosophical inquiry enjoys within this wing of mediaeval Judaism, we can then understand some of the restlessness of his questions about predestination and, indeed, the range of his questions about other perplexing and mysterious aspects of Christianity. If all of these are revealed truths, — Calavera probably believes this — they too must be susceptible to some sort of rational explanation, and it is virtually our religious duty to search for them. Incidentally, when we speak of the "rationalism" of Lando, we have in mind much the same thing as these intellectual tendencies in Calavera. The difference between them is that whereas Lando, with his ranging mind, actually succeeds in reducing certain Christian notions, Grace, for example, to a sort of rational explanation, Calavera is often content to ask questions merely. The difference is, I think, very significant.

CALAVERA: FAITH AND DOUBT

Calavera seems to thrive on dilemma. Even when great religious issues are not involved, he seems to show in his poems a real fondness for balancing arguments *pro* and *con* and leaving the question he is dealing with undecided. One composition of his is a delightful piece addressed to Love, in which the poet solemnly rehearses to him all the arguments men offer in his favor, then all the arguments to the contrary. The poet concludes the work by himself withholding judgment.[51] Another interesting work of Calavera is a debate between an eager knight and an unwilling lady — the piece is a one-man *tenson,* appropriately. The gentleman presses his none too honorable suit: the lady remains an exemplar of purity. The work is clearly meant to be an edifying piece, and yet, the poet does not deal unkindly with the disappointed lover. The last octave spoken by him allows him a last angry word, plausible, not un-human.

> "Agora vos digo que puedo, señora,
> Contar vos por mas cruel é mas dura
> De cuantas conosco en el mundo agora
> Nin se fallar puede en toda scritura.
> Do la al diablo atanta cordura;
> Syenpre desides al omme de non;
> Mas fortalesa teneys que Sanson:
> Con vos non me vale rrason nin mesura."[52]

Calavera's fondness for debate was not entirely a literary affair. We can find him at odds with himself — in debate with himself, really — as we read several of his poems on a single subject. The great theme of the *contemptus mundi,* for example, the single subject most easy to associate with Calavera, is subject, over the whole spread of his work, to two mutually exclusive interpretations. On one hand, it is no problem to find poems by him on the transitoriness of things on earth, on the veleities of Fortune, all sorts of *contemptus mundi* topics, allied to thoroughly

---
[51] CB 534.
[52] CB 538.

Christian reflections on Eternal Life, on the need of turning from sin, if we are to be rewarded hereafter, and the rest. [53] All such poems, original as they may be, fall well within the pattern of a Christian commonplace. On the other hand we are confronted with a Work like the following in which many of these familiar Christian landmarks are missing:

> Tan poca es commo sy fuese ninguna
> La vida del mundo en que bevimos,
> Non sabe donde ymos nin donde venimos
> El viejo, el moço, el ninno de cuna;
> Todo es sueño é sonbra de luna
> Salvo el tienpo en que á Dios loamos,
> E todo lo al es burla en que andamos
> Enbueltos en calma syguyendo fortuna.
>
> Dyuso del cielo omme non alcança
> Tal çertydunbre, nin ay tan perfeto
> Que bien me desclare aqueste secreto;
> De los pasados, sy ay rremenbrança,
> Desque van, non torrnan contar su estança
> Nin viene jamas avisar sus amigos,
> Non vemos salvo los dichos antigos
> E fé que tenemos con firme esperança.
>
> Todo el mundo es ser opyniones,
> Enpero que lançan todos á un fyto:
> Bestias é aves fasta el mosquito
> Nasçen é mueren, segunt los varones;
> Fuelgan muy ledos los sus coraçones
> De los ommes synples é torpes, pesados;
> Los entendidos é agudos letrados
> Penan é amargan las sus entençiones.
>
> Los sessos humanos non çesan urdiendo,
> Texendo é fasiendo obras de arañas,
> Al cabo se fallan mas vanos que cañas
> E tengo que de'sto se está Dios rryendo:
> El que mas trabaja pensando é leyendo
> De'ste paño vyste mas corto pedaço,
> Que todo es ello mirar por çedaço. [54]

---

[53] CB 530, 532 could be called *contemptus mundi* poems which are doctrinally Christian.

[54] CB 531.

The poem's one identifiably Christian feature is the fleeting reference to Faith and Hope at the end of the second stanza. All else is Jewish, the mood, the theme, aspects of the language. By Jewish in this case we mean culturally Jewish, not so specifically with regard to religion. The work reflects certain features, the skepticism, the pessimism, and a few determinated ideas current among cultivated Jews in Spain during the late Middle Ages. Two of these, virtually present, give us a special clue to the world of ideas underlying the work. These are: the denial of Providence in the sublunary world and the denial of personal immortality. The presence in the poem of the first of these can be gathered from its whole drift. There is the line about God's mockery of the world, for example — "tengo que de'sto se está Dios rryendo", as well as the notion that all time not spent in the praise of God is worthless. We need only contrast Calavera here to Manrique's line in which the world is good insofar as men make good use of it. Most significant of all, the whole rosary of gloomy thoughts strung out in Calavera's poem includes the reflection that there is no certainty beneath the spheres ("Dyuso del cielo" &c.). The denial of immortality is found in the lines beginning "Todo el mundo...". In both these cases I would also suppose that the skepticism of the poem is as evident from what it leaves out as by what it states. To express doubts about the world-order or about immortality without any sort of mitigating statement is itself significant.

Now both of these views — the denial of Providence beneath the sphere of the moon, and the denial of immortality — are bag and baggage of Jewish thought and sentiment of more or less philosophic type. They can be found, first of all, in formal philosophical literature. Calavera's line that below heaven there is no certainty is found in nearly all Jewish philosophy from before Maimonides down to the poet's own time. Providence extends through the spheres down to genera and species on earth, that is, to the general order of the laws of nature, but by no means to the individuals within the species, much less to single events on earth:

> In the lower or sublunary portion of the Universe Providence does not extend to the individual members of

species...I do not believe that it is through the interference of Divine Providence that a certain leaf drops, nor do I hold that when a certain spider catches a certain fly, that this is the special result of a special decree and will of God in that moment. [55]

So speaks Maimonides. The number of hairs on our heads is not numbered. The indifference of the world-order to man is especially stressed by some writers. The Toledan philosopher, ibn Crispin, a late Averroist, echoes a commonplace in denying that Providence consists in rewards and punishments within this life. The stars distribute favors and troubles to men without regard to merit. [56] The Catalan rabbi, Joseph ben Shalom Ashkenazy, a Cabalist, and a declared enemy of philosophy, accuses philosophers of teaching this doctrine. [57]

In the case of personal immortality too we can appeal to a sort of common teaching on the part of philosophers. In this case, however, there is a certain variety of emphasis. Nearly all from Abraham ben Ezra on are agreed that the Active Intellect is one for all men (this is in contrast to the Christian scholastics, who teach that every man possesses his own active intellect), and that what immortality the human soul has resides in this sort of over-soul. Though this doctrine would seem to do away immediately with the possibility of personal survival, some writers did attempt to make some provision for it. In any case, however, the doctrine of the unity of the Active Intellect provided a flimsy basis for individual immortality, and in fact many Jews denied it flatly. [58]

---

[55] *Guide*, III, 16, pp. 286-287.
[56] For ibn Crispin, see Vajda, "A propos", p. 28.
[57] G. Vajda, "Un chapitre", p. 95.
[58] The notion that the Agent Intellect is one for all men is virtually common property among Jewish philosophers. Any handbook gives details about this problem, e.g., I. Husik, *History*, or Vajda, *Introduction*. See also above, note 23 of this chapter. Jews who were skeptics in religious matters denied all forms of personal survival. Among theologians, strictly speaking, however, Maimonides distinguishes himself by virtually denying that there was to be a future resurrection: this is the burden of J. Finkel's article, "Maimonides's Treatise on the Resurrection, a Comparative Study", in *Essays on Maimonides* (New York, 1941). Saadia, Crescas and Albó held that the resurrection was a doctrine of Judaism, but was not a *fundamental* doctrine [*Jewish Encyclopedia*, Article "Resurrection" (New York, 1905), X, 384].

Now these two doctrines also had resonance beyond the philosopher's study. Polemic, for example, is a good witness to their currency. Alfonso de Valladolid, in his all-important list of Jewish beliefs, includes a number of philosophical ideas, among which we can find traces of the notions sketched above of Providence and immortality. [59] Much more interesting and revealing, perhaps, is a passage in a work dating from the late fourteenth century by a Spanish Jewish polemicist, Semtob ben Isaac Shaprid, in which he attacks the skeptic, superficial and facile student of philosophy. In this extraordinary list of grievances he attributes to his opponent the general proposition that God did things badly, nothing less. This gloomy philosopher paraphrased by Semtob cites as examples the ills of pregnancy and the pangs of childbirth, which lead women to hate their children. Children, he goes on, are a perennial torment to their parents. Fathers are put to such pains to provide for them. Their diseases during infancy are sources of anxiety. The awakening of sensuality during adolescence is a further trial. Grown men are assailed by the desire for riches, and are plagued by the fear of the loss of their fortunes. Finally, of course, death consumes us all, bringing our labor to naught. All of this chaos in human life is compounded by the fact that there is no after-life where the just are rewarded and the unjust punished. Very significantly with respect to Calavera, this grim passage is all couched in the phrases of Koheleth, proclaiming vanity. We recall that the poem we are discussing is a veritable rosary of thoughts from the Preacher. [60]

Once more on the matter of Providence, we find that in a work as familiar as the proverbs of Semtob of Carrión, the theme of the indifference of the world and the heavens to man and his doings is a very prominent feature. Here is a well-known passage:

---

[59] See note 36.

[60] I. Loeb, "Polémistes", p. 224. This treatise dates from the years 1380-1385. J. Millás Vallicrosa includes in *La sagrada poesía hebraicoespañola* a composition from about this time by one Selomó ben Měšal-lam de Piera, which, similar in theme to the Calavera piece, is also full of echoes of Ecclesiastes.

> El mundo non tyen ojo,
> Nin entyende fazer
> Avn omne enojo
> E aotro plazer.
> Razonal cada vno
> Segunt la su fazyenda,
> E non ha con ninguno
> Amistad nin contyenda:
> Nin se paga nin se ensaña,
> Nin ama nin desama,
> Nin ha ninguna maña,
> Nin rresponde nin llama. &c. [61]

Summing up, we could say that the Jews of more or less philosophic persuasion, in confronting the apparent lack of purpose in the world, were lacking two important props which would have kept them from falling into such deep anxiety or bitterness, props available to the believing Christian, for example. One was the supposition that every single occurrence in the world, the fall of every sparrow, was looked over by divine Providence. The other was the belief that this life, with all its chances, is the preparation for another, which is more perfect, more permanent, and in no way subject to change or contradiction. Calavera, for the moment, at least felt himself to be without these props, and the urgency and the dark mood of his poem is due in great part to this lack.

The study of the above poem has revealed to us a most significant fact: Calavera could, at different moments of his life, write poems which express belief, and poems which express doubt, lines full of Christian sentiments, and lines almost devoid of them. Two different outlooks on life may well have been constantly before his mind. There was no element of caprice in this: we gather as much from a single work of his in which the two viewpoints confront each other. [62] This extraordinary poem is one of his lengthiest; it too is on the vanity of human wishes. It is in the form of a long exchange between the poet and God. After a brief introduction Calavera addresses an extensive complaint to

---

[61] Santob de Carrión, *Proverbios morales*, ed. I. González Llubera (Cambridge, Eng., 1947), p. 145. A. Castro comments on lines in the *Proverbios* similar to these in *La realidad histórica de España* (México, 1954).
[62] CB 529.

God on the injustices of fortune; to this an unseen voice answers, in some detail, in God's name. Some of the material in the complaint is topical, of course. The following should be familiar to readers of the *Cancionero* or the *Rimado de palacio* as it dwells on the discrepancy between merit and reward:

> ...A los servidores veo señores,
> E los señores son servidores,
> Açores grajean é los cuervos caçan.
>
> Veo los nobles andar por mal cabo,
> Los synples alcançan honrras, ofiçios,
> Los nesçios honrrados en sus benefiçios,
> Doctores muy pobres andan en su cabo:
> Buen omme de armas non alcança rrasion,
> Peligra inocente por grande ocassyon,
> E muere en su cama provado ladron
> El malo ha buen fyn, el justo mal cabo. &c.

These lines occur fairly late in the poem, however. The *opening* deals with the poor condition of his mule:

> De Madrit partiendo con el Rrey en febrero
> Por yr aguardando la su grant mesnada,
> Llegando á Ssegovia fallé en mi posada
> Bien coxa mi mula, lyssiada de vero,
> E avia perdido otra en dos messes
> E al libramiento ponien me rrevesses;
> Tenia de francos é doblas jaqueses,
> Florines é blancas vasio el esquero.
>
> Tenia de camino leguas setenta,
> Con este cuydado luego en proviso
> Se rrepresentó delante mi vysso
> En quanto trabajo, afan é tormenta
> Anda mi vida; &c.

There is nothing "literary" about these ills. The fact is that the bulk of the "complaint", everything, really, up to the passage quoted above is made up of a list of completely personal troubles. He complains that he is hounded by misfortune while others live surrounded by every earthly pleasure, honors, the most splendid luxury. He complains of perennial poverty:

> Yo antes que tenga diez francos enteros
> Por mas que quatorse estó ya adebdado,
> Segunt los diablos fuyen de sagrado
> Asy de mi arca fuyen los dineros; [63]

and that God gives him only the desire for worldly goods and nothing more:

> De casas, viñas é plata, heredades
> Solo el deseo, Señor, vos me dades... [64]

All his business ventures come to naught. His service to his superiors gains him nothing while others less zealous get along very well. In a word, the topical complaint concerning fortune comes only at the climax of this section of the poem: it is borne up by a good deal of autobiography, as it were. Without indulging in fatuous biography-writing it seems safe to say that all this personal matter, the two mules, the seventy leagues' journey, and so on, gives the work a very un-topical urgency, and a sense of Calavera's intimate involvement with questions of fortune and Providence; the topic has been brought to life. What we said earlier about Lando's intrusion into his own poem applies here, *mutatis mutandis,* to the wealth of personal anecdote. The fortune question for Calavera is "vivida por la persona total": it is not theoretical, merely. We are not here claiming great things for Calavera the poet, but simply stressing the fact that this question — like the predestination question and others — is a genuine personal issue for Calavera, the man, and not simply a poetic posture.

The poet's speech concludes as he calls God to account for all these apparent injustices, the while protesting his fidelity to Him:

> E pues que notorio é sobre natura,
> Señor, es el vuestro absoluto poder,
> Fasedme por vuestra merçed entender
> Aquesta ordenança que tanto es escura:

---

[63] I am not suggesting at this point that the complaints about poverty were not topical in the Middle Ages.
[64] CB 529.

> De aquestos rreveses que yo vo tomando
> Presumo de vos manera de vando,
> Pero aquesto digo, Señor, protestando
> Tener lo que tiene la santa Escritura.

The old theme of God's fundamental injustice, which as we recall was at the heart of Calavera's predestination question, is also at the heart of this one. That he should formulate the fortune question as he does once more clearly shows how close he is to his Jewish roots, especially as regards the notion of Providence. The rationalist Judaism of Calavera's time, as we have insisted, is not very familiar with the idea that God's decrees pervade the whole fabric of the world, down to the smallest detail. Such must have been one of the most disquieting doctrines he encountered in his new religion, and this passage, characteristically, shows him drawing the most radical and discomforting conclusions from it.

The second section of the poem, like the first, on the whole seems to follow few stereotypes. The speech of the unseen voice, God's advocate, composed as it is of arguments drawn from a variety of sources, Biblical, Boethian, of the author's invention, presents as a whole a very curious and original character, very personal, at once naïve and searching. The topics the speaker touches on in order to edify and console the poet run all the way from high religious wisdom to counsels of rather gross human prudence. On one hand, he is reminded that God chastens those He loves and means to favor, that earthly goods are harmful to us as we pursue heaven, and that it is madness to desire them, that they are contemptible compared to the permanent goods of heaven. Poverty, the voice goes on, is a sure path to blessedness, and was consecrated by Christ's companionship with her for thirty-two years. Joined to these thoughts are others less purely spiritual: the wealthy and the highly placed are assailed by cares from which the poor are exempt. Less high-minded than even this is the thought that there are always people whose fortunes are worse than ours. Notwithstanding these last, however, the tone of the speech is grave and lofty, at once Biblical and Boethian-Stoic.

All this matter is but a preface to the poet's absolutely central and fundamental thought, expressed at the end of the voice's speech:

"Lo al que paresçe non ser bien fecho
En los tus ojos, segunt la ordenança,
En Dios es ello muy syn errança,
Syn ningunt daño, con todo provecho:
Aunque esto su sseso non puede alcançar,
Devries una cosa tu consyderar,
Qu'el juez que es justo non deve judgar
Salvo justicia, razon é derecho.

"Sy desto demandas la çertenidat
De todo en todo, dime tú luego
Por qual manera quanto con el fuego
Dios da la calor é la sequedat,
E la umidat con la calentura,
El humido frio con frio se cura;
E faz me tú çierto por qual fygura
La lus fué partida de la escuridat.

"O qué tales son aquellos çimientos
Que sostienen la tierra, el ayre, el çielo, &c.

The paraphrase of the passage from the book of Job is most appropriate. Calavera's solution to questions of fortune and Providence is to throw them all into the realm of mystery, of the secrets of God. In other words, the original dilemma is to a considerable extent simply left standing. Thus Calavera's poem is radically different from one on a similar theme by Fernán Pérez de Guzmán, *Dezir contra los que dizen que Dios en este mundo nin da bien por bien nin mal por mal* (formidable title!).[65] In this work the poet, basing himself on a chapter of the *De civitate Dei*, relates the sufferings in the world immediately to the great scheme of election: trials edify the just and further the ruin of the reprobate. Likewise, within the confines of the *Baena*, Fray Alfonso de la Monja, a Dominican, composes a *respuesta* on fortune addressed to Imperial, in which, in a Boethian mood, he gives her a nature, mutability, and declares her to be a part of God's will.[66] It matters very little what we think of these solutions, whether we think they are good or not, or whether we believe that as explana-

---

[65] In Foulché Delbosc, *Cancionero castellano del siglo XV*, NBAE 19 (Madrid, 1912), I, 650.
[66] CB 246.

tion they are only delaying the inevitable appeal to mystery. The fact is that these and others have attempted to formulate and verbalize solutions to the fortune question in some form and that Calavera, in sharp contrast, has given us what is virtually no explanation at all. Strong as his belief may be, it opens no paths in his mind, at least not in this case. As far as rational and articulated theories are concerned, the state of the question is exactly the same before and after the formidable soulsearching.

The importance of this fact cannot be overestimated. It lights up two significant areas well worth exploring, one related to thought and sentiment in fifteenth century Spain in general, the other having to do with Calavera himself. In the first place, our Comendador comes close to being the ideal paradigm of the exceedingly familiar type of the *converso* turned Christian Stoic. It is well known that Stoicism, or *senequismo* was a *converso* characteristic; from the time of Alonso de Cartagena to that of Rojas, many of the great writers on Stoic themes in Spain were either men of Jewish origin or were strongly influenced by such.[67] It seems to me entirely plausible that one of the reasons such a tradition might have arisen is to be found in the absence in certain kinds of Judaism of a clear notion of Providence as all-pervading. It is not unbelievable that men whose philosophy of life consisted in a withdrawal, through spirit, from the flow of events, of a search for exemption, through virtue and the mind, from the buffets of life might have been led to such a philosophy by a tradition which saw little order in this flow, little system in the life. In Calavera we see this happening in its simplest and purest form. His memories of Judaism are vivid and extensive. Confronted by the Christian view of Providence, he accepts it, but with perplexity, as it were. And simultaneously he accepts

---

[67] The rôle of the *converso* Alonso de Cartagena as schoolmaster to a whole generation of Castilian writers of importance is described in J. Marichal, *La voluntad de estilo* (Barcelona, 1957). Mena is the author of *Coplas que fizo el famoso Juan de Mena contra los pecados mortales* (Foulché, I, 120) of strong stoical flavor. Senecan also the *Diálogo e razonamiento sobre la muerte del Marqués de Santillana* by Pero Díaz de Toledo, as are others of his works. Fray Hernando de Talavera speaks of "el católico filósofo Séneca" in *Como se ha de ordenar el tiempo* (in *Escritores místicos españoles*, p. 95). Cf. A. Castro, *op. cit.*, pp. 549-550.

more or less Stoic solutions to his life-problems. In the case of later *converso* writers matters are somewhat complicated by the fact that often their memories of the old religion were either scant or nonexistent. It is also true that in many cases they were men of considerably more reading and sophistication, and so would be less likely to be as satisfied with as simple and blunt non-explanations as is Calavera. Their situation is nevertheless much the same as his. The rationalist Jewish view of Providence ceases in their day to be a doctrine and becomes simply a mood, and the choice of Stoic solutions still remains its consequence.

Calavera's refusal to advance or repeat theories about the goodness of Providence has also, of course, hugely important implications with respect to his own range of ideas. We return at this point to our original question of the sincerity of the Christian faith of this and other *conversos* among this group of poets. Calavera's faith is genuinely "agonic," if we may use the expression. Without in the least meaning to attribute to him a complexity of spirit more typical of the twentieth century than of the fifteenth, we may say that his is a "faith which doubts," or to put it more gently, "a faith which accepts difficulties." When he accepts the idea of the all-pervasive goodness of Providence, but refuses to subject it to any kind of reasoning, we must conclude that many of his old perplexities are still with him. Our picture of Calavera's "rationalism" is thus completed. We find him here pursuing his scrutiny of the data of revelation, continuing to believe in the revelation even when the pursuit yields negative results. In a way, then, Calavera conforms to a type of person not uncommon in the Jewish community, the "Averroist," so called, the man who cannot trust reason to confirm revelation, but who somehow manages to keep faith with both. Calavera believes in God's justice even when reason takes the devil's part. His faith is tried, but it is not therefore false.

Calavera has a formula in which he expresses his agonic faith: it is a turn of phrase which occurs too often to be an accident. Whenever he airs one of his serious doubts, he never fails to add that he wishes and means to believe and teach nothing but what the True Faith teaches, and that his questions are not meant to be violations of that faith. Thus in the poem we have just been studying he says at the end of his complaint, after having suspected God of being party to his sufferings:

> Pero aquesto digo, Señor, protestando
> Tener lo que tiene la santa Escritura.

Likewise in the last stanza of the *pregunta* based on Jewish polemic he says:

> Segunt la Yglesia lo manda creer,
> Yo creo esto todo [the Trinity, the Incarnation &c.]
>   muy sinplemente...

The cliché occurs twice in the predestination series; the first time is in the *finida* of the original question:

> Señor, esto digo so protestaçion
> Que mi entinçion es querer disputar,
> Mas non poner dubda nin faser errar,
> Que Dios que es justo non puede judgar
> Salvante derecho, justiçia, rrazon.

The second example is in the final *respuesta*, which as we recall is also by Calavera:

> Todos aquellos quantos trataron
> En esta muy fuerte, escura quistion,
> Sy con synplesa algunos dubdaron,
> En lo qu'es mi culpa, demando perdon:
> En esta materia mi imaginaçion
> Fué con letrados atanto arguyr,
> Fasta la pura verdat esprimir
> Guardando de yerro el mi coraçon.

Taking these protestations of orthodoxy and good faith in isolation, one might be tempted to read them as pure formula. But if we see them in the context of the whole thought and sentiment of Calavera, we have little reason to doubt that they are sincere, and that they express his meaning exactly.

A CHRISTIAN RABBI?

We conclude this examination of the direct influence of Jewish ideas on the poets included in *Baena* by examining the poem which perhaps displays its Jewish background most prominently and obviously. This is a work by one Garçi Alvarez de Alarcón, a poet not otherwise represented in the collection, or elsewhere, to my knowledge. The poem is the sixth of the seven answers addressed to Calavera in response to his predestination *pregunta*. At the very heart of his argument are two topics obviously drawn from the Jewish philosophical tradition: one of these is garnished with what seems to be a verbal reminiscence of Maimonides. Nowhere in the collection is this sort of matter so thinly disguised. Once again this is probably not a case of bad faith; Alarcón is in all likelihood a convinced Christian, as much so as the odd intellectual climate would permit. The undisguised origin of his ideas is rather a commentary, as is the case in so many other instances, on the poet's inability to digest very much theology at short notice, on his unfamiliarity with things Christian due to the recentness of his conversion.

We recall the main drift of Calavera's argument as we saw it in his *pregunta* to Ayala: God, in creating a man He infallibly knows is eventually going to Hell, is a party to evil, is indeed the source of evil. Alarcón's answer to this difficulty is simple and astonishing. God simply does not know beforehand which man will be saved and which not. This strange solution, unheard of in Christian theology, nevertheless does indeed break down into certain elements familiar to philosophical Jews, as we will see. The argument moves through three stages. The first of these is the proposition that God does not know particulars:

> Saber acabado é poder conplido
> Syn contradiçion en Dios es por çierto,
> Mas es por tal guisa á nos encubierto
> Que lo non alcançar pudo omme nasçido;
> Syn conparaçion de todo sentido
> Sabe todas cossas ansy en general,
> Que desir non se puede por espeçial
> Assy commo sson é sseran é han seydo.

Incurren en pena muy grave por esto
Los á tal saber dan conparaçion,
Pues en vos es mengua é en Dios perfeçion
Ser su saber synple é non ser conpuesto: &c. [68]

This matter derives from Avicenna, who is readily available to fifteenth century Jews through Hebrew translations. Also it is repeated with little change by several Jewish authors, both by those who hold this doctrine, like Gersonides, and by those who dissent from it, like Albalag. Avicenna teaches that God's knowledge of the world is limited to a knowledge or genera and species, and does not include a knowledge of individuals as such. This does not imply a defect in His knowledge: on the contrary, it assures us of its perfection, unsullied as it is with perishable things, with multiplicity:

> Just as it would mean attributing a defect to the necessary Being to say that He performs many different acts, so also that He performs many intellections [Avicenna supposes that many individuals can only be grasped by as many intellections]; but on the contrary, the necessary Being understands nothing except in a universal way. [69]

There is no need to trace the history of this idea within the Jewish camp. Suffice it to point out that in questions concerning divine knowledge Jewish and Arab philosophers are divided. Averroes and Maimonides say that it does include individuals as such; Avicenna, ibn Daud and Gersonides say it does not. [70] Naturally the matter is of sufficient importance so that not infrequently philosophers dealing with it take full note of the alternative they do not accept. All this is by way of saying that there

---

[68] CB 523.

[69] My translation, from *Avicennae metaphysices compendium*, trans. N. Carame (Rome, 1926), p. 121. This is a translation of *Al-Najat*. On the existence of Hebrew translations of Avicenna see *Universal Jewish Encyclopedia* (New York, 1939), article "Avicenna".

[70] Abraham ibn David treats free will in *Emunah Ramah*, Tract. II, principle 6, Chap. 2, quoted in Fleg, II, 50-52; Gersonides, in *Milhamot*, III, Chap. 1-6, pp. 120-150 (reference in a note in I. Husik, *History;* Husik paraphrases this section on pp. 340-345). Maimonides deals with God's knowledge of particulars in *Guide*, III, 20-21, pp. 292-296. G. Vajda ("A propos," p. 24) surveys different views on this problem.

is not the least difficulty in explaining the presence of this particular solution in Alarcón. The matter is discussed in many works perfectly accessible to him.

The next few lines in the same passage are the ones which suggest that its author was acquainted with Maimonides. He quotes Isaias:

> Por el profeta se dis magnifiesto [sic]
> Vuestros pensamientos nin las vuestras vias
> Non pueden ser tales commo las mias,
> Muy bien se entiende syn glosa el testo.

The *Moreh* also quotes Isaias LV: 8, also in a passage on the radical unlikeness of human knowledge and divine. Here is the immediate context:

> ...there is an essential distinction between His knowledge and ours, like the distinction between the substance of the heavens and that of the earth. The *Prophets* have *clearly* expressed this. Comp. 'For my thoughts...' [71]

There is a curious complication here in the fact that the doctrine Alarcón enunciates is not Maimonidean. But it is also quite possible that he is simply paraphrasing the *Guide* on the subject of the disparity of the two kinds of knowledge, a notion our poet in general accepts, though not in the form in which Maimonides formulates it.

The doctrine of God's ignorance of particulars is for Alarcón an assurance to us of His justice in saving some men and damning others:

> Aun mas vos digo que puesto que viesse
> Dios por nostra via qual serie dañoso,
> Ante que nasçiesse é fuesse engendrado
> E de lo criar çessar se quisiesse,
> Serie grant rrason que lo non fisiese
> Por que su çiençia seria ffallida,
> Sy desta manera non fuesse conplida,
> Segunt que primero preçita la oviesse.

---

[71] The underscorings are mine. *Guide*, III, 20, p. 294.

> La grant Providençia de la Trenidat
> Quiso por esso de su condiçion
> Dar nos alvedrio é deliberaçion
> Para escoger bondat ó mal,
> E ssaber non quisso la espeçialidat
> De los que sse salvan ó se han de dapnar,
> Por que á los malos pueda condenar
> E salvar los buenos la ssu piedat.
>
> Valor asy mesmo con tal puridat
> De saber Dios quiso tener apartado,
> Que non se falle en cuerpo criado
> Nin de otro lo oviesse la ssu Deydat, &c.

He continues by drawing the conclusion, in answer to Calavera, that performing meritorious acts of devotion is not lost effort nullified by God's prior resolutions, but that they do further our salvation.

This very peculiar, barely plausible argument has in it one element which is, in fact, moderately reasonable. This is the proposition implied and expressed in the passage which says that if we accept God's ignorance of particulars, we will have no difficulty in accepting also man's free will. Now this landmark of rationality on a rather chaotic landscape is again a prominent theme in some Jewish philosophers. Gersonides, for example, values his own theory of the divine knowledge among other reasons because it saves human freedom. Ibn Daud builds a whole development on the subject of future contingents and of God's ignorance of them apparently with the express purpose of justifying belief in free will. The two elements in the Alarcón poem, then, which make some sense and show some philosophical sophistication are derived from matter available and current in Jewish philosophy. His borrowings are, to be sure, not taken from the "common stock" of this body of thought, that fund of common doctrines which perennially appear in Jewish thought. His statements definitively separate him from some thinkers and ally him to others, and these alignments cannot fail to be interesting. But on the other hand there is absolutely nothing original in the

Jewish side of his thinking: both these steps in his argument can be traced to well established traditions. [72]

There remains the unpleasant residue of his argument, the specifically Christian portion of it. We follow the poet with cautious respect as he tells us that God knows only the general order of the universe and not particular beings and events as such. We find it not completely absurd of him to say that the truth of this proposition insures the possibility of free will. But how is it possible to draw a doctrine of salvation and damnation out of all this? If God is ignorant of the details of men's conduct, how can He reward the good with Heaven and punish the sinful with Hell? The awkwardness of this point of the reasoning did not escape the author. He confronts his difficulty manfully, but throws everything back into confusion:

> Qu'él [God] sabe los salvos é los condenados
> Quien fueron é son é seran é quales,
> Por tan exçelentes cursos divinales
> Que son ya del todo á nos ocultados.

Like Calavera on Providence, Alarcón throws his whole problem into the realm of mystery. In this case, however, the mystery, the gap in our understanding, is not provided for in his system of articulated ideas. It is not much of a success, even as an appeal to mystery. It is hard to imagine what he means.

We see, then, that Alarcón proceeds securely as long as he is on the familiar territory of Jewish philosophy, and that he stumbles miserably as he passes to Christian theology. *Mutatis mutandis*, something like this could be said of many of our *Baena* poets, converts of a few years, not familiar with the new religion. The particular reason for the anomalies in Alarcón's argument are also easy to find. As we already know, the notions of salvation, damnation, of Heaven and Hell, are utterly alien to the ideas of philosophical Judaism and are far from typical of the beliefs of

---

[72] Needless to say, after 1277 a Christian theologian would not permit himself positions of this sort (see note 25). I think that we can dismiss the possibility of a Latin Averroist influence here. As we stated, Latin Averroists are uncommon in Spain, and in any case, Averroism is an academic phenomenon, and there is little to suggest that Alarcón was a university man.

other traditions in mediaeval Jewry. What the poet has tried to do is simply to solve a typical problem in Christian theology, drawing exclusively from the arsenal of Jewish philosophy. It is obvious that he is well grounded in the latter, and it is equally obvious that it does not supply him with the arguments he needs. The little repertory of ideas about God's relation to the natural order and about man's place in that order are not of much use in discussing Grace and election. It is a long leap from genera and species to the rôle of free will in predestination.

Actually, Alarcón has no illusions about his powers as a theologian. His poem is generously garnished with expressions of humility like the following, all of which may be absolutely sincere:

> Yo pido por merçed en forma devida
> E á los mis mayores de sabiduria,
> Que cunpla mi mengua la su teologia
> Con puro amor de graçia escogida;

* * *

> A mí me cunpliera por ende callar
> Ante que tentar en tan alto grado,
> E bien lo faria, mas es me forçado,
> Que la verdat pura me fase fablar,
> Rrogando á Dios que me guarde de errar
> E con omildat pidiendo liçençia,
> A los mis mayores de grant sapiençia,
> Por que mi rrespuesta pueda mejor dar.

In still another passage he suggests that Pero López de Ayala, who, he insists, is vastly more skilled in these matters than he, be also entrusted with the task of framing an answer: thus Ayala will supply his own considerable defects. All of this in terms of the poem means simply that he is knowingly framing a provisional, tentative answer. He is in no sense attempting, like Alfonso de la Torre, author of the *Vision delectable,* deliberately to create a system which somehow harmonizes Jewish and Christian elements. Neither is he trying to make some sort of synthesis of Christian faith and Jewish wisdom, like the great scholastics. He is simply setting out to solve a Christian theological problem out of the only fund of religious thinking he knows, which happens to be Jewish.

Be it noted, incidentally, that the man Garçi Alvarez de Alarcón is not completely unknown to us, and that what information about him we do possess is not out of consonance with what the poem tells us. There is good reason to believe that he is identical with the Garçi Alvarez de Alarcón who stood at the side of Jerónimo de Santa Fé, the brilliant and fanatical Christian apologist at the dispute of Tortosa in 1413. Alarcón was nothing less than a converted rabbi, a man of great Biblical and Talmudic learning. This rabbinic learning naturally made him very useful in disputes with Jews, such as this one. It appears that aside from his rôle at Tortosa, he was a zealous apostle, and succeeded in bringing many Jews to Christianity. [73] It is not unbelievable that this is the same person as our poet. The latter's erudition in things Jewish is considerable, vastly greater, for example, than that of any of the other poets we have discussed. It is also true that in the list of poets who answered Calavera's *pregunta* he is in the company of men with a reputation for theological learning, Pero López de Ayala, Fray Alonso de Medina, whose prominence in the Hieronymite order we read of in Sigüenza. His own importance as a convert well schooled in rabbinic lore, and as a learned apologist might have won him his place on the list. It could be added that one of the other two "non-poets" in the series, Fray Alonso, was a man with an independent reputation as a theologian.

The one fact which makes it hard to believe that the poet is identical to the apologist at Tortosa is the poorness of the poet's theology. How was it possible for a person known to be a skillful polemicist to be so ignorant of learned Christian thought in areas as important as those which are touched on in the poem to Calavera? And yet, this difficulty disappears, if we are aware of the character of Christian anti-Jewish polemic of this time, especially as it might be practiced by one familiar with rabbinic literature. [74] Much of the body of the traditional arguments in this polemic is quite devoid of theological complexity, for one thing. Much of it centered on the question of the messiahship of Christ: "Art thou he who is to come, or shall we look for another?" The proof

---

[73] J. Amador de los Ríos, *Estudios sobre los judíos* (Madrid, 1864), p. 328.

[74] Baer, *op. cit.*, p. 311.

that the Messiah had indeed come depended, naturally enough, on the testimony of the Talmud. Nearly every Christian anti-Jewish treatise from the thirteenth century through the fifteenth and beyond contains a collection of Talmudic *loci*, which, to the satisfaction of some, appeared to prove that the Messiah had already been born, and that Christ was he. Given this dependence on the Talmud, it is easy to see the tremendous usefulness of a converted rabbi as a disputant. Such a person would be in a good position to use these arguments against men also learned in Bible and Talmud, and since the arguments principally dealt with questions of fact and not of doctrine, we can understand how the apologist need not have been very learned in the latter. It is ironical to think that such a man need not have known theology, but might also have been forced by the exigencies of the apostleship to keep alive his Jewish learning.

THE CONVERSOS IN THE 'CANCIONERO DE BAENA'

So we conclude our study of the direct influence of Judaism upon certain poets included in *Baena*. Perhaps the most obvious thing that has come to light in this review is the fact that for many of the poets of early fifteenth century Castile Judaism and Jewish memories lay not very far below the surface, and that they are not impossible to discover in their writings. This is a way of saying the obvious, that their conversion did not entail sudden changes of ideas, opinions or sentiments on the part of any of them. There was no miraculous transformation that made these men exactly like their Old Christian neighbors. Whatever the pressure on them might have been, they could not forget completely their Jewish religious heritage. We remind ourselves in passing that this is not necessarily a reflection on their sincerity as Christians.

All this wealth of Jewish memories is striking for its variety in *converso* literature. Though it is absurdly easy to find evidence of the presence of Judaizers on the Spanish scene, it is by no means so easy to find traces of Judaism in formal literature, poetry, serious treatises, "essays," and the rest. The most famous work of this century that does show Jewish influence is the *Vision delectable* of Alfonso de la Torre, large parts of which are simply translations of portions of Maimonides' *Guide*.[75] There are not many more examples. This singularity of the *Baena* material is certainly one of its great points of interest.

It possesses others. To my mind the clear, unmistakable presence of Judaism in the writings of the *Baena* poets is exceedingly valuable as a vantage point in studying literature by *conversos* who do not show this specifically Jewish influence. We would propose a new approach in the study of the intellectual and spiritual history of the Judeo-Christians. It has been usual, in discussing them and the traits they have in common, the ideas they tend to share, to appeal to social forces, collective psychological factors, or to certain non-religious, non-doctrinal Jewish traditions, and treat *them* as the decisive formative elements. A new, rather specialized procedure would be to examine the influence of ideas and doctrinal traditions which come out of a strictly Jewish milieu on the first generation of *conversos,* and then to trace the influence of the ideas of these men on subsequent generations. This is what we have attempted to do as we suggested that the choice of *senequismo* as a philosophy of life in the fifteenth century by certain persons can be traced to certain Jewish attitudes towards Providence. The possibilities do not end here. It might prove feasible, for example, to find out the origin of other *converso* intellectual postures in the Jewish rationalism we have described. One field in which our new approach would surely prove fruitful is the presence among many Spaniards of the mood of fatalism in regard to the moral life. I am thinking of the unusual emphasis placed at this time on the influence of temperament, sometimes thought to be decisive, on our moral goodness, or our lack of it. The vulgar form of this attitude, the one attacked by the Archpriest of Talavera, is the one which says that moral effort is useless, since we are good or bad by nature.[76] A more sophisticated version is Talavera's own, that temperament inclines one strongly, but that at critical moments the inclination can be re-

---

[75] J. P. Wickersham Crawford, "The *Visión delectable* of Alfonso de la Torre and Maimonides, *Guide for the Perplexed*," *PMLA*, XXVIII, 2, pp. 188-212.

[76] *El Arcipreste de Talavera*, pp. 341-348.

sisted. Though this sort of idea is by no means absent from mediaeval Christian literature, it is uttered with more frankness and less caution by Jewish authors. Maimonides has this to say, for example:

> Many men are naturally so constituted that all perfection is impossible; i. e., he whose heart is very warm and is himself very powerful, is very sure to be passionate, though he tries to counteract that disposition by training; he whose testicles are warm, humid and vigorous, and the organs connected therewith are surcharged, will not easily refrain from sin, even if he makes great efforts to restrain himself. You also find persons of great levity and rashness, whose excited manners and wild gestures prove that their constitution is in disorder, and their temperament so bad that it cannot be cured. Such persons can never attain to perfection &c. [77]

It seems far from impossible that the study of the writings of men who were undoubtedly acquainted with this theme in Judaism might well explain in detail its prominence on the Christian scene.

Properly explained, then, the *Cancionero de Baena* might well prove to contain a matrix of germ ideas for the study of *converso* life and letters, in the sense that the Judeo-Christians whose work appears there in every sense straddle two worlds, being at once acquainted from birth with Judaism and firmly established in the Christian world. The particular structuring of ideas and opinions in these men becomes an exportable item, so to speak, is something that with certain modifications can be adopted by later generations. One word of caution, however. Many of the attitudes maintained by the *Baena* poets are, without the least question, doomed to disappear soon, notably the cavalier and naïve approach

---

[77] *Guide*, I, 34, p. 47. The determinism, or near determinism in the moral order that we speak of is, of course, quite different from the *total* determinism propounded by some of the late scholastics, Bradwardine, Autrecourt, and finally Wyclif. Our determinism is grounded in the physical character of the universe, the influence of the spheres on the sublunar world. Determination by *temperament* is the moral side of the matter. The later schoolmen conceived determinism on rather different grounds from these [cf. L. Baudry, *La querelle des futurs contingents* (Paris, 1950) and C. Michalski, "Le problème de la volonté à Oxford et à Paris au XIVe siècle," in *Studia Philosophica* (Leopoli, 1937), II, 233-364].

to theology, for example. One problem that scholarship might consider taking seriously is precisely the question of what attitudes of these men were destined to survive, and which not, which notions and sentiments are simply results of a particular situation and of a particular moment of history and which are to have resonance beyond that moment. Such studies will undoubtedly clear up a good many dark areas in fifteenth century Castilian literature.

Chapter II

"LA POESÍA ES UNA GRAÇIA INFUSA DEL SEÑOR DIOS"

In the study which follows we will discuss the view held by some of the *enriqueño* poets that the art of poetry is acquired only through the grace of God, "por graçia infusa del señor Dios".[1] As we will see, this theory is at once a rather specialized doctrine of poetic inspiration and an apology for ignorance, for the poet's lack of learning. What it really claims is that poets are especially empowered to speak of the things of God, even though they know no theology; their peculiar gift permits them to compete with learned men, indeed to surpass them. The importance of the idea for our generation of poets can be gauged by the fact that Baena, the compiler of the *Cancionero,* mentions it in a conspicuous place in the prologue of his collection. This prose piece on the high purpose of letters in general and of poetry in particular says of the latter that

> la qual çiençia [the art of poetry, the gaya çiençia] é avisaçion é dotrina que della depende é es avida é rreçebida é alcançada por graçia infusa del señor Dios...

This statement of the case, complete as it is, extending divine inspiration not only to the art of poetry, but also to its content, is certainly in a prominent place in the collection, in this introductory essay. It is well, then, for us to remind ourselves in this regard of how Baena stands with respect to his collection. We

---

[1] Baena's prologue, p. 9.

recall that the *Cancionero de Baena* was compiled for John II between 1440 and 1460,[2] a good many years after many of the pieces in it were composed. Baena himself was one of a group of poets represented in it which was active in the very first years of the century. To the extent, then, that the prologue is not a mere formality, that its author shows any candor, its ideas represent in some sense what he recalls at a distance of some forty years as the important ideas and principles that underlay the poetic practice of the group. It is especially striking that this *graçia* passage is the only one in the prologue which reflects directly and clearly matter in the collection itself: we know that grace and poetry are explicitly associated in some of the poems. It is perfectly clear, therefore, that Baena, at once collector and contributor, thought that the grace idea was an important one for his collection, and that, of the whole repertory of ideas current in his group, this was the one most worth repeating.

Before we start to examine our texts and to explore the doctrine and the ways our poets understood it, it is well that we explore the background of this strange notion. The likeliest is that the theory is an original application of the Franciscan, vaguely Joachimite notion that God enlightens His simple followers directly in such a way as to confound the wise of the world. As we shall see, explicit utterance is given this idea several times in the *Cancionero de Baena,* mainly in the mouths of Lando and Villasandino. An idea akin to this, the notion that Grace's function is principally that of illuminating, is perhaps somewhat more widespread. Lando, once again, says of his contemporary, St. Vincent Ferrer: "bive *alunbrado* de graçya divina."[3] Likewise, Fernán Sánchez Calavera has this to say in his poem on predestination:

>...tengo que estos á quien *resplandores*
>De graçia alunbram con forma apuesta,
>En alguna cosa son meresçedores...[4]

---

[2] H. R. Lang, *The 'Cancionero de Baena' Reproduced from the Unique Manuscript in the Bibliothèque Nationale,* foreword by H. R. Lang (New York, 1926), p. 24.
[3] CB 287.
[4] CB 525.

Useless to stress the Franciscan-Spiritual, Joachimite pedigree of these ideas. The superiority of the simple over the wise is a common notion among radical Franciscan writers and their allies: so also is the strong hostility for speculation, especially for scholasticism.[5] This distaste for scholastic philosophy and theology is, of course, basic to the poetic-grace theory, as we shall see. Also characteristically Spiritual-Franciscan-Joachimite is the belief that the faithful are enlightened directly by the Holy Ghost, this, the mark of a new aeon.[6]

We must not imagine that these are the only themes in the *Cancionero* of radical Franciscan origin. Prophecy, for example, beloved of Friars Minor,[7] plays an important part in the intellectual world of some of our poets. Significantly, a number of the prophetic poems in the collection show the direct influence of John of Rupescissa, well-known French Franciscan and prophet of the fourteenth century. John was a defender of strict observance of the Franciscan rule, and was deeply influenced by writers of strongly Joachimite stamp.[8] Another Franciscan theme, the

---

[5] In radical Franciscan writings it is a common notion that the Spiritual Church is made up of the simple and untutored, that the learned are in league with Babylon. A good index to the prevalence of this attitude is to be found in the writings of the Inquisitor Eymerich (for whom, to be sure, Spirituals, Beguins, Lullists, and Michaelists tend to fade into one another): he registers it as one of the opinions of one of these undifferentiated species of his that theologians of this time are powerless to enunciate and explain the mysteries of Christian doctrine [cf. P. Roura Roca, *La posición doctrinal de fray Nicolás Eymerich, O. P. en la polémica luliana* (Gerona, 1959)]. The illuminist trend prominent in the ideology of so many radical Franciscans [discussed at length in E. Benz, *Ecclesia Spiritualis* (Stuttgart, 1934), pp. 276 ff.] of course goes hand in hand with the contempt for speculation.

[6] See preceding note.

[7] As is well known, the radical or "Spiritual" Franciscan outlook as early as the thirteenth century became wedded to Joachimism, and Joachimism is, as it were, a philosophy of history, a theology in which prophecy plays a central rôle. The work of Peter John Olivi is perhaps the most notable of many instances of the integration of Franciscan history and ideals into a Joachimite framework [cf. R. Manselli, *La "Lectura in Apocalypsim" di Pietro di Giovanni Olivi* (Rome, 1955).] A good account of the circulation of prophetistic and Joachimite and Olivian matter in more or less Franciscan circles may be found in R. Manselli, *Spirituali e beghini in Provenza* (Rome, 1959).

[8] The prophecy, for example, that the King of Castile will conquer the Moslems throughout the world and will be crowned Emperor in Jerusalem (CB 199, by Villasandino, and CB 335, by Gonçalo Martínez de Medina)

attack on the wealth and worldliness of prelates, is also to be found in the *Baena* collection, in this case in two anonymous poems.[9] Thus we have not the least difficulty in supposing that radical Franciscan ideas were known to our poets, or that the poetic-grace theory grows out of some of these ideas.

It may seem to some readers that we have made matters altogether too complicated. The fact is that the poetic-grace theory is apparently fully tagged and identified by one of the poets of the collection. Fray Lope del Monte, a Franciscan (a Conventual, that is, also a scholastic, and no friend of "Spirituals" or illuminists) accuses Lando of speaking like a follower of Llull. Lando, in a verse addressed to the friar, has in effect boasted of his poetico-theological powers, adding:

> Que Dios sus secretos quiso rrevelar
> A parvulos synples, pessados é rrudos;
> E á los prudentes dexalos desnudos,

Fray Lope's answer runs:

> Fablar de escripturas quando contesçiere,
> Yo non contradigo con lengua sepista,
> Nin yo menoscabo al que bien dixere,
> Quando quier que sea pequeño legista:
> Pero sy me fabla de Rremon Lulista,
> Sofryr non me cunple sus dechos çeviles,

He continues some lines further on:

> Nunca vy ssecretos de Dios en ditar [10]

---

is a modification of an important prophecy of Rupescissa — made by him concerning the King of France, incidentally [cf. J. R. Vademecum, quoted and paraphrased in J. Pou y Martí, *Visionarios, beguinos y fraticelos catalanes* (Vich, 1930), pp. 304 ff.]. An excellent general study of the life and prophetic works of Rupescissa is: J. Bignanni-Odier, *Études sur Jean de Roquetaillade* (Paris, 1952).

[9] CB 115, anon. and CB 340, also anon., but included among the poems of Gonçalo Martínez de Medina. The special emphasis made by the Spirituals on poverty is at one with the condemnation of wealthy prelates: poverty is the mark of the Spiritual Church, and wealthy churchmen the mark of the Carnal Church (cf. Manselli, *La "Lectura"*, pp. 203ff.).

[10] Lando's *pregunta* is CB 272, Fray Lope's answer, CB 273.

So he makes it clear that he had versifiers in mind. He concludes by saying that the mysteries of God are simply not within the reach of the unlearned.

So it is, then, that this complex of ideas, the enlightening of the simple by God, the helplessness of the learned, the putting of theology into verse, all this is identified as Lullian. The great problem, however, lies in the fact that none of these ideas has very much connection with the thinker Llull as we know him today. What is more, Lando's random thoughts on religion and philosophy, as far as I can see, have little resemblance to the teachings of the Doctor Illuminatus. So on the face of it, the epithet "Lulista," far from clearing up the problem of sources simply saddles us with further questions.

To my mind, the most plausible resolution of this paradox lies in the fact that the Lullian tradition in the Peninsula — which is a strong one in the fourteenth and fifteenth centuries — actually comes to harbor a number of illuminist, Joachimite, radical Franciscan elements. The method and doctrines of Llull are a divine revelation, infinitely more precious than the teaching of the schools. The appearance in the world of Llull inaugurates a third and final aeon in the history of the world, this one under the special guidance of the Holy Ghost, just as the Old Testament had been under the Father, the New, under the Son. Llull was, in fact, a Franciscan tertiary. We must bear in mind also, of course, that Lullism, Joachimite or not, was among other things a popular doctrine, a method or dialectic which put all the secrets of theology within the reach of comparatively unlearned people. [11] Paradoxically, then, something which history judges to be one of the great philosophical and theological systems of the Middle Ages passed in the eyes of many as a species of "wisdom of the simple," a wisdom to confound the subtlety of the schools. In this sense, therefore, we can see in part why it might have struck Fray Lope to accuse Lando of being a Lullian, even though the content and style of his theology, so to speak, has very little to do with the content and style of that of the historical Llull.

---

[11] For the fusion of Lullism and radical Franciscan ideas see J. and T. Carreras y Artau, *Historia de la filosofía española: filosofía cristiana de los siglos XIII al XV* (Madrid, 1939), II, 32-43.

To sum up, then, the radical Franciscan ancestry of the poetry-grace idea seems clear. The epithet "Lulista" applied to it by one of its critics is in the long run a confirmation of this background, not a denial.

We will now attempt to define the scope of the poetry-grace idea within the writings of our generation of poets. In the whole bulk of the *Cancionero* we find the word *graçia* used in connection with poetry a scant four times. To this meager list we may add a few passages where the idea that poetry is a gift from above is clearly expressed. This rather slim amount of evidence gives a poor idea of the importance of the notion. It is altogether notable, for example, that Baena, as we have pointed out, places the idea at the very head of his collection, in the prologue. The very importance he, the compiler, puts on the poetry-grace idea suggests that we do well to look for traces of this strange doctrine over a fairly wide front.

In order, therefore, to discover what the poetry-grace theory actually meant to some of our poets, we must examine some of the works that in one way or another attempt to expound this original poetics. We will find it most convenient to do so under two general headings, what we might call an external account of the doctrine and an internal. In the first case, we must look at the texts which tell us what sort of poet is supposed to possess the special gift of grace, what his qualifications must be and in the second, we must try to discover the inner structure of the presumed grace.

In its external aspect the grace doctrine seems to be two things. It is at once a justification of the poet's ignorance — a basis for holding learning in contempt — and a ground for valuing technique over other poetic qualities. This is what seems to be the use of the word *graçia* in the following verses of Villasandino:

> A mí bien me plaze por que se estienda
> La gaya çiençia en boca de tales
> Que sean donossos fydalgos...
> E troben limado syn pavor de emienda;
> Mas pues que los torpes ya sueltan la rryenda,
> Quemen sus libros do quiera que son
> Virgilio é Dante, Oraçio é Platon,
> E otros poetas que diz la leyenda.

"LA POESIA ES UNA GRAÇIA INFUSA DEL SEÑOR DIOS"   69

> Aqui todo bueno su sesso despienda,
> E juntense algunos de los naturales,
> Legos é artistas é retorycales
> Que han é ovieron onrrossa bivienda;
> Apaguen tal fuego por que non se ençienda
> Mandando que callen aquellos que non
> Resçiben por graçia divina este don
> De la poetria: todo omme lo entienda. &c. [12]

"Virgilio é Dante" and the rest are, I take it, in apposition with "libros"; the subject of "quemen" is "torpes," understood. The "legos," "artistas" and "retorycales" are, of course, holders of academic titles or degrees awarded by some sort of poetic academy like the Consistory of Toulouse or that of Barcelona. [13] Villasandino in speaking of the "artistas" and so on is thinking simply of what these "Provençal" academies might teach: he is thinking of men who can manage the intricacies of rhyme and meter, subtleties well known to later Provençal poets and to himself, as he often boasts. We know that this is his drift because whenever he exalts technical facility — something he does often — he submerges the reader in a welter of professional vocabulary taken from Provençal. Thus, in an exchange of poems with Lando of which poetic grace is more or less the subject, Villasandino accuses the *converso* poet of ineptness in versification in the Provençal mode, and overwhelms him with just such a storm of technical terms:

> E pues vos tenedes por tan sabidor
> Que en tan breve tienpo tan alto sobistes,
> So maravillado commo preposystes
> Syn lay é syn deslay, syn cor syn discor,
> Syn doble man sobre sensillo ó menor,
> Syn encadenado dexar ó prender,
> Que arte comun devedes creer
> Que non tiene en sy saber nin valor. [14]

To the technically apt, Provençal-style troubadours he opposes learned poets, those whose works are heavy with bookish learning,

---

[12] CB 80.
[13] Cf. J. Rubió Balaguer, article on Catalan literature in *Historia general de las literaturas hispánicas* (Madrid, 1949), I, 726.
[14] CB 255.

with commonplaces drawn from grave authors. We can be in little doubt that the poets he is thinking of are Imperial and his followers. He practically tells us so in one text. The opposition between technically facile and learned poets is of course perennial in Villasandino: he seems particularly fond of accusing Lando of being in the latter class — this is the point of the passage above quoted. But another such piece addressed to Fernán Manuel accuses him flatly of being a follower of the transplanted Italian, on precisely these grounds. He concludes:

> Pues çeñides la correa
> De Françisco Ynperial,
> Vestra arte tal ó qual
> Ya sé de qué pie coxquea. [15]

Thus the division of poets into learned and facile is not academic, but on the contrary absolutely timely.

We may line up, then, the two opposing camps in Villasandino's poem. On one hand there are the poets who follow more or less Provençal patterns: for these, training and formation is schooling in *technique*, and these are the ones who are favored by Heaven. On the other hand there are those whose background and formation is erudition; these adorn their works with examples, anecdotes, *sententiae* drawn from the "classics," old and new. Villasandino clarifies the status of the "graçia divina" in that he associates it entirely with the poets who like himself are more concerned with technique than with grave *auctores*. For him, inspiration and technical proficiency go hand in hand. This is apparently a fairly constant element in the conception of poetic grace. It is present in Baena's all-important prologue where, as we recall, he states that the science of poetry and its high content is given the poet:

> ...por graçia infusa del señor Dios que la da é la enbya é influye en aquel ó aquellos que byen é sabya é sotyl é derechamente la saben fazer é ordenar é conponer é limar é escandir é medir por sus piés é pausas, é por sus consonantes é sylabas é açentos, é por artes sotiles é de muy diversas é syngulares nonbranças, &c. [16]

---

[15] CB 258.
[16] The prologue, once more, pp. 9-10.

Thus, in the Villasandino poem we have a suggestion of an "external" definition of poetic grace — the poet's charisma is somehow simultaneous with technical facility — and we see that the grace is thought of as a superior alternative to *literary* erudition. The poet's inspired invention is opposed to the weighty *literary* reading that gives another sort of versifier his supposed authority.

Lando, in his utterances on poetic grace, opposes the poet's gift to another sort of erudition, the theological and canonical learning of the schoolmen. As we have seen, this opposition is the theme of the exchange of verses between him and Fray Lope del Monte.

> ...muchos letrados é frayles faldudos
> Metrifican prossas de ynota color,
> Mas non tienen graçia qu'es vertut mayor
> E fablan syn orden commo tartamudos.
>
> Non sean por esto algunos sañudos
> Que graçia es magna que enbia el Señor,
> E non por ciençia de ningunt dotor
> Nin de los que cantan en sus estornudos. [17]

Lando is not thinking here only of the ineptitude of the *letrados* as writers of verse. The whole argument in the exchange is built around Lando's boast that he can outdo even Fray Lope in theology. In the first *pregunta* addressed by Lando to the friar, the latter is asked, ironically, of course, for a lesson. Should Lando answer very securely to this teaching, however, Fray Lope must not be surprised:

> Aun que vos seades famoso jurysta,
> Sabed que delante de sabios sotyles,
> Ya fise yo prosas por actos gentiles,
> Maguer non so alto nin lyndo partysta.
>
> Mas por aquesto non deven tomar
> Enbidia los grandes dotores sesudos,
> Que Dios sus secretos quiso rrevelar
> A parvulos synples, pessados é rrudos;
> E á los prudentes dexalos desnudos, &c.[18]

---

[17] CB 274.
[18] CB 272.

This is, of course, the passage on the enlightening of the simple which we examined before. In it Lando makes it clear, as the Villasandino verses just quoted do not, that poetic grace is indeed a sort of private revelation, that it conveys some kind of knowledge. Like Villasandino, however, Lando makes the special gift the exclusive possession of those who know the ins and outs of writing verse, something he says clerical poets are at a loss to do well.

Villasandino opposes poetic grace to the learning of the Imperialesque poets; Lando opposes it to the learning of theologians and canonists. Other things separate them as well: Villasandino often boasts that he is more immersed in Provençal poetic lore than Lando. It is clear, however, that they are fundamentally of one mind as far as the poetic grace idea is concerned. This is evident particularly in an exchange of *respuestas* between the two poets, something we could irreverently call an argument as to who is the more inspired. Lando boasts of his powers as a theologian:

> Desde el çielo de la luna
> Contenplad fasta el abismo,
> Que yo vos daré inforismo
> De rrason sotyl alguna,
> Syn tomar rregla ninguna
> De maestro nin doctor,
> Salvo graçia del Señor
> Que rreyna sobre fortuna.
>
> Mas arryba non subades
> Un punto por cortesya,
> Pues yo non sé theologia
> Nin las sus abtoridades.
> Por sy argumentades
> Alguna dubda muy fonda,
> Bien podrá ser que rresponda
> Mejor que vos non cuydades. [19]

The context of this utterance is most revealing. Several poems back in the exchange, Lando makes a similar boast of his powers.

---

[19] CB 257.

Villasandino counters it by saying that Lando may well excel in learning and theological culture, but that he is his inferior in the art of poetry. Lando then, in this poem, claims with distinct pride an ignorance equal to his rival's, and appealing to the principle of grace to which they both subscribe, declares himself able to beat Villasandino at his own game.

Externally considered, then, it is clear that poetic grace is supposed to be a substitute for learning and consequently a sanction for ignorance, and that it is the exclusive property of technically facile poets. Turning to other matters, we must now try to discover what the inner make-up of this special gift to poets is thought to be. Here we will once again find Lando's utterances on the subject most revealing. In the exchange with Villasandino, Lando's first poem, full of irony as it is, directed very specifically at his fellow poet, turns out to be the most useful and complete statement of the doctrine of poetic grace which we have examined to date. He leads us along familiar paths as he gives us again the enlightening of the simple by God:

> Ca Dios rreparte sus dones
> A todos, segunt leemos,
> E por el Apostol veemos
> Provadas estas rrasones.
> Los de rrudos coraçones
> A las veses disen tanto,
> Que algunt doctor muy santo
> Non funda tales questiones.
> ...Commo fiyso á vos dyleto,
> Profundo de grant saber,
> Bien assy pudo faser
> Otro mucho mas discreto. &c. [20]

The crucial thing here is that Lando is at once describing himself as "discreto" and "de rrudo coraçon." It is useless to say that the passage is merely malicious and ironical; it is a fact that both rudeness and intelligence are in some way the two faces of the grace idea. This rudeness, in the first place, is the correlative of enlightenment: it is the simple whom God enlightens. And yet

---

[20] CB 253.

paradoxically, it is the intelligent person who can speak great wisdom taught by no earthly authorities at all, only by God Himself. The person's native wit is what makes up for his lack of learning. We must take both parts of Lando's statement at face value, and not dismiss one of them for the sake of some specious clarity.

Discreto is, without question, a key word in the above quotation. The word *graçia* as used by Villasandino, Lando or Baena means simply a kind of native wit, what later generations would call "ingenio." Most characteristically, it means a sort of native wit at once able to deal with grave religious problems and with the intricacies of writing verse. Lando's words to Fray Lope, in which he claims superiority to the Franciscan both as theologian and composer of verses, are exactly to this point. So also is the passage quoted above from Baena's prologue in which it is made clear that both the art of poetry, the "çiençia," and the "avisaçion é dotrina que della depende" come from the grace of God. The "çiençia" is beyond any doubt the craft of making verses: grace is the influence behind those who

> byen é sabya é sotyl é derechamente la saben fazer é ordenar é conponer é limar é escandir é medir por sus piés é pausas, é por sus consonantes é sylabas é açentos, &c. [21]

That in broader terms *graçia* is equivalent to *ingenio* is borne witness to by Fernando de la Torre, a writer who flourished some fifty years after the composition of some of our poems, but who was well acquainted with the literature of his century, and who knew the *Baena* material very well. He devotes a lengthy essay to the relative usefulness of learning and untutored wit for a person who writes. [22] We also know from his own words that in stating the case for *ingenio* he has before him the words and example of Lando and Villasandino, who, as he says, excelled as poets even though they were "sin letras". In other words, Torre

---

[21] The prologue, pp. 9-10.
[22] *Cancionero y obras en prosa de Fernando de la Torre*, ed. Paz y Meliá (Dresden, 1907), pp. 49-57.

must certainly have known their grace-theory, and may very well have been influenced by it as he formulated his own views about the place of "ingenio" in literature. The only reason he translates *graçia* by *ingenio* is that the "sectarian" connections of the former word — Spiritual ideas about the enlightening of the faithful — were either of no interest to him, or, what is more likely, were completely unknown to him.

The most accurate commentary on the meaning of the word *graçia*, and indeed the best testimony to the very considerable portée of the idea is the actual body of poems in which the poet's prerogative to speak out on weighty and subtle questions is actually exercised. Which ones are these? Our immediate temptation would be to include every poem written within the Baena-Lando-Villasandino circle on a vaguely theological subject. If we excluded works by clerics from the list, and for reasons we will give shortly, added Imperial's works to it, such would not be a bad guess. But within this larger group of poems there is a smaller group which are consciously and deliberately written to prove the theory right. It is one thing for Lando and Imperial to write simple doctrinal poems about predestination in answer to a question of Calavera, and quite another for Lando, for example, to match his skill at theologizing with some *letrado* with the express purpose of showing that an untutored poet *can* teach high doctrine. In the latter case we can see the grace-theory pretty much in the foreground of the discussion, even if it is not mentioned explicitly. In the other case we see the theory making its presence felt, to be sure, but in the background, implicit in the fact of the poet's speech.

As we read over these "inspired" works in search of illuminist doctrine, we may be surprised to find in them so little that could be called mystical, mysterious, or even in some vague romantic sense "poetic". The apparent prosiness of these pieces should not disconcert us. It is true that if we except the handful of prophetic poems, strictly speaking, we seem to find little in the collection that is in the least visionary. In all these works, which range all the way from riddle solutions to elaborate doctrinal statements, there is hardly one utterance which is not discursive, rational, unambiguous. It could even be said that in some instances the doctrinal matter, isolated from the question of poetic grace, has nothing in its internal make-up to reveal it to be the invention of poets specifically. Lando's views on predestination may be good or bad theology, they may be orthodox or heretical; as ideas simply, as theory, they seem hardly more "poetic" in any sense than those, say, of Fray Alonso de Medina, a professional theologian. Likewise Francisco Imperial and Lando in astrologizing Fortune are not being more poetic than Fray Diego de Valencia, who holds very different views. It is quite true that secular poets in the collection tend to teach a different set of doctrines from those of the schoolmen-friars, but this is clearly for reasons external to the ideas themselves.

However, we must put all of these works in their true setting. With regard to the *purely* doctrinal pieces, we may suppose that their poets thought grace operative in simply the fact that they were able to speak at all of the things of God, this in spite of their lack of learning or of their authority as teachers. Without too much irony we could describe the grace-idea in this case as a "mechanical" theory of inspiration, the notion that a poet's opinion carries weight simply because he is a poet. Works in this mode are more interesting for their content than for their poetics and there is no special need to discuss them at this point. They are easy enough to identify: Imperial on the seven virtues and on the birth of Prince John, both Imperial and Lando on predestination, other works of Lando of a moral and doctrinal character, and so forth.

It is the other sort of poem, however, the kind in which poetic grace is in some sense an issue, that we begin to learn more fully what is really meant by *graçia* and in what sense it is illumination. In a word, it could be said that the doctrine we draw from these pieces is more or less as follows: the poet's technical proficiency, combined with his native wit, prepares him to receive certain flashes of divine inspiration, and the natural gifts and attainments are precisely the *medium* through which the divine influx expresses itself. For a good example of all this in action we turn once again to Lando in his exchange with Fray Lope del Monte. In this *tenson,* as we recall, poetic grace was the very subject at hand. In the *finida* of the original *pregunta* by Lando we are given a brief and ingenious summary of the doctrine of the Trinity; speaking of the fact that God enlightens the simple, Lando says:

> Ca él solo fase fablar á los mudos
> E veer á los çiegos en claro tenor,
> Con sabiduria, poder é amor,
> De una sustançia unida syn nudos. [23]

The huge importance for us of these lines can be made clear only if we fit them into the context of the *pregunta* as a whole. As we recall, the piece begins as Lando ironically asks Fray Lope for a lesson in theology. The friar must not show surprise, however, if his pupil answers very well; learned or not, he has already written many verses to very high purpose. It is also useless for the learned to show envy for such as him, for God reveals His secrets to the simple, and leaves the wise unenlightened. Thoughts on the mercy of the Triune God end the poem, as we have seen.

It is absolutely clear that Lando meant the final little flurry of *ingenio* on the Trinity to be a modest sample of his prowess as a theologian. He designates the three Persons each by an epithet, and suggests the mode of Their Unity by a bright metaphor — "without knots." All of this sounds like a humble sort of home-made theology. The thing to be noted, however, above all is that it is theology executed through *poetic means*. The wit involved is generally a poetic quality, and is particularly so as it shows itself in an interesting choice of metaphors and other figures. Wit, however, leads a double life, and seems to point to a broader range of its own power. Wit, *ingenio*, a poetic quality, is also exceedingly useful in the solving of mysteries. Thus *ingenious* persons can understand riddles, are not at a loss to sort out deceitful appearances, can see instantly what is hidden from less subtle spirits. The Trinity is a mystery — for Lando, at least, so I should guess — in just this sense. At this point, let us forget all we may know learned theology says about the inaccessibility of the Trinity to rational scrutiny. We must, without irreverence, rather think of the Trinity as a sort of super-conundrum: how can What is One be also Three? Lando must have thought of it that way, the more so, since he was born and possibly brought up a Jew. It might be added that Jewish polemic tends to treat the doctrine of Trinity in just these very simple terms.[24] Thus we are finally

---
[23] CB 272.
[24] See the preceding study in this volume.

clear about what sort of illumination from above we have in mind in speaking of poetic grace. It is the "stroke" of wit, the momentary flash of intelligence which in an instant can see the solution to a puzzle, can fathom "mysteries" less absolute than the Triune God. So at last our total doctrine emerges. The "graçia infusa del señor Dios" is *ingenio,* something which is at once the poet's chief ornament, and the key to the solving of mysteries, those of Scripture and Revelation as well as others. This, then, is the modification a Spiritual idea undergoes at the hands of the *Baena* poets.

So it is that Lando, once again, is of the greatest help to us in clarifying our notion of *graçia.* It is Villasandino, however, who in all the collection gives us the greatest number of poems intended to prove the validity of the idea, and it is to him we must turn next for light. In order to understand how the problem of poetic grace comes up in his poems, we must realize that he is, in the eyes of some of his fellow poets, the bearer par excellence of the grace doctrine. It is significant, for example, that Baena, the anthologist, himself connects poetic grace to him in an important way. In all of Baena's brief epigraphs which introduce the works of the various poets, the grace idea is mentioned only once: this is in his piece on Villasandino:

> el qual por graçia infusa que Dios en él puso, fué esmalte é lus é espejo é corona é monarca de todos los poetas é trovadores que fasta oy fueron en toda España. [25]

Fernán Pérez de Guzmán also makes reference only twice in his early poems to the fact that the art of poetry gives the poet a right to treat lofty themes: both times he is almost certainly addressing Villasandino (certainly in one case, nearly so in the other). Then too, only his close association with the grace idea in the eyes of others could explain the curious fact that he alone, of all the poets of the collection, has questions put to him by clerics on religious matters. The clerics in *Baena,* as might be expected, have little sympathy for the idea of poetic grace. One could hardly expect champions of orthodoxy to show interest in doctrine so manifestly Spiritual. It is also possible that Villasan-

---

[25] This epigraph precedes CB 1.

dino was known to them in general as a person of questionable orthodoxy: certainly what we know about him would confirm this possibility. Finally, the poetry-grace idea was, in a sense, a weapon forged against them, and against their formal learning in divinity. The one reason, then, why the clerics should single out Villasandino for special treatment is that they are in effect attacking him and his theory, and are trying to hold both up to ridicule.

They *do* put him to the test, in any event. In a way which should not at this point surprise us in the least, the questions he is most often subjected to are little more than riddles and puzzles. In every way typical of these *preguntas* are a whole series addressed to him by an anonymous *bachiller* from Salamanca. The first of these opens with a piece of mock-flattery:

> Non tengo que syente la naturaleza
> Nin puedo ssentyr en sy la razon
> De omme prudente de grant discreçion,
> Que menor de otro le sobre en alteza;
> Pero yo bien creo de çierta fyrmeza
> Que menor de angel le puja en estado:
> Deseo ssaber d'algunt grant letrado
> Quien es que meresçe aver tal franqueza. [26]

"Letrado" is, of course, ironical and malicious: Villasandino boasts very little learning, much less a university title. The *bachiller* goes on to ask in this omnibus *pregunta*:

> ...¿commo podria estar engendrado
> Un padre syn dubda de su fija pura?

Questions like this fill up two more stanzas: he asks who the father is who cannot beget a son while he is alive, but who at death is able to do so. And so other questions. Villasandino is, of course, equal to all of this. He answers that Christ as a man is lower than the angels, yet surpasses them by virtue of His divinity. Mary, the Mother of God, is, of course, daughter of her own Son (this is a commonplace in the Liturgy). Finally, "unless

---

[26] CB 84.

the grain of wheat falls into the ground and dies, it remains alone. But if it dies, it brings forth much fruit": this verse paraphrased supplies the answer to the riddle about the father and his son.

It should be clear that we are moving on the same territory mapped out in connection with Lando's verses on the Trinity. What is being put to the test, *ingenio,* wit, fundamentally, is something of both poetic and religious significance. Wit is the poet's chief ornament in general, as we have often repeated. The solving of riddles, however, has special significance in that it is a *conventional* test of the poet's power. This is a Provençal pattern, of course; the *Leys d'amor* provide recipes for the asking of riddles in verse.[27] This pattern is not absent elsewhere in the *Cancionero de Baena*: Villasandino himself is the author of several riddles.[28] The religious angle is scarcely more complicated. The riddles, all on religious themes, are, once again, small "mysteries," divine conundrums the quick-witted and inspired can unravel in an instant. This is all clearly within the scope of poetic grace, a special light to search out the dark things of God. We may add to this the fact that two of the riddles are based directly on Holy Scripture. We must remember that a recurring theme in Spiritual thought is the notion that the mark of the spiritual man is ability to understand Scripture, aided by no one except the Holy Spirit.

Thus, the scope of the first question and answer is fairly clear-cut. But the exchange goes on, and Villasandino is asked questions of a very different character. In the next piece, the *bachiller* asks him what death is, and wherein lies its justice in the order of things, death which consumes great and small, weak and strong. Villasandino, answering, draws rather conventional edification from the thought of death: it should spur us to repent and lead good Christian lives:

> ...fue la persona del Padre repissa
> Porque fyzo al mundo muger nin varon;
> Assy quantos fueron é serán é son
> Pagaron é pagan esta amarga ssyssa.

---

[27] *Leys d'amor,* ed. Anglade, II, 157, "Cobla divinativa."
[28] CB 132, 133, 134, 135.

> Por ende, amigo, todo omme se escude
> Con la penitençia, sy muerte barrunta,
> Contryçion con obra seya luego junta
> De la ley de Christo jamas non se mude;
> De mal penssamiento luego se desnude,
> El tal será salvo, en esto me fundo; [29]

The *bachiller* then passes from a question of moral import to one of speculative. Who, the cleric asks, is the mover of the first sphere? Who is able to move anything so large? This Villasandino answers with a certain caution:

> ...es un secreto d'escura carrera
> Del Alto syn fyn...
> Que este secreto es del que non miente
> E sobre natura inpera viviente,
> Potestad divina, lus clara é apuesta: [30]

Now, what is to be noted here is that in these two sets of questions and answers, unlike the first, there is no particular sort of poetic *skill* being put to the test. Thus, the answers are by far more interesting for their content than for any sort of poetic device that is applied, or for the presence of any sort of facility or ingenuity, such as, say, the ability to solve riddles. In other words, if they are "poetic" at all, they are so on the basis of our "mechanical" theory of inspiration; they are full of weighty doctrine simply because a poet wrote them. They are not, therefore, what the Lando piece on the Trinity is: a theological problem solved by "poetic" means.

Now, what, if anything, do we learn about the supposed powers of poets in this oddly assorted series of questions and answers? If we take this group as a whole, we may find them very illuminating in this regard. Each of the three questions corresponds to a well-established and more or less generally recognized realm in which the poet claims authority. These are: the sphere of ingeniosity, the moral, and the speculative. Of the first, we need add nothing here. As regards the moral sphere, we may say that it

---

[29] CB 87.
[30] CB 89.

is perfectly clear that poets at this time regarded moral teaching as one of their functions. The great number of poems on edifying subjects in *Baena,* poems on Fortune, on Death, is witness to this, and the impressive example and strong influence of Pero López de Ayala, poetic moralist par excellence, whose works were undoubtedly read by some of our group of poets, must not be underestimated. Later Provençal poetry also abounds in moral themes.[31] As far as poetry on speculative subjects is concerned, our poets had the example (perhaps grounded on legend) of Dante, combined with the more immediate example and practice of Imperial, who was the bearer of all the wisdom of Italy. The cleric tests all three of these claims of the poet. Now in two of these areas, the moral and the speculative, it might be reasonably doubted that poets are the ones best equipped to deal with them, poets as opposed to men of learning, for example. The third area, wit, is indeed a poet's home ground, but wit turned onto the theological subject matter in a sense is treated as something new and questionable.[32] The test, therefore, to which the *Bachiller* sub-

---

[31] The *Leys d'amor* makes much of the moral purpose of poetry, especially in the chapter on rhetoric [*Leys d'amor,* ed. J. Anglade (Toulouse, 1919), I, 71ff.]. There is no need to stress the prominence of moral themes in later Provençal poetry; however, a good example of the sort of moralizing poet who might have been known to the *enriqueño* group might be the Valencian, Pere March (father of Auzias, no less!), who scarcely wrote a line without moralizing intent [see A. Pagès, *Les "Coblas" ou les poésies lyriques provenço-catalanes de Jacme, Pere, et Arnau March* (Toulouse, 1949).]

[32] W. Ong has pointed out that among some of the great mediaeval liturgical poets wit of various sorts is the normal means used for the expressing of theological mysteries. The practical coincidence between this element in hymnody and the ways of the *Baena* poets is very strong. Is there a relationship of cause and effect? Did Lando, Villasandino and the rest know the hymns of the liturgy well enough to take note of this aspect in them? It is interesting to note that Fernán Pérez de Guzmán cites the hymnody of St. Thomas as proof that poetry is a divine science:

> Que el trobar sea un saber divino
> Asás se demuestra en muchos lugares;
> ...E el doctor santo fray Tomas de Aquino,
> En aquel devoto é notable yno
> Del qual la Yglesia tanta mencion fase;

Pérez de Guzmán, however, is a somewhat more broadly read poet than some of his older contemporaries. In the case of a Lando or a Villasandino it would be very unwise to affirm positively that they were seriously influenced by Latin hymnody.

jects Villasandino follows a fairly logical order. Wit, a quality all hands can agree is fundamental to a poet, comes first. The point at issue is whether wit can also be thought of as a divine spark, enabling men to fathom the mysteries of Christianity. To be sure, the content of the riddles is "theological" in a fairly trivial way: the religious subject matter may have been little more than a token. It is clear nevertheless that the double function of wit, the poetic, and the religious, was the real target in the first pair of poems. Having explored this matter, the cleric then goes on to see whether the presence in a man of wit or "grace" really entitles him to deal with graver moral and philosophical questions. Therefore he asks him a pair of questions which on the face of them do not require a witty or "poetic" answer at all: they could be answered as well by a theologian or a philosopher as by a poet. What we have here, then, is an instance of the grace theory being put to a complete test. Its basic thesis, we recall, is that poets, unlearned though they be, can beat *letrados* at their own game. Once the *bachiller* has established that Villasandino indeed possesses qualities proper to a poet, he goes on to test him in areas where he cannot rely at all on his poetic tricks or his wit, where he must perform exactly as a theologian would, that, or else fail the test. This exchange, then, puts the problem of poetic grace in a somewhat different light from that in which Lando leaves it. The *bachiller* in his test in effect analyzes it, breaks it down into its parts. Wit, *ingenio*, is seen as its basis, but the poet's ability to theologize is tested separately. A clearer picture of the supposed gift emerges, in that emphasis is placed on the poet's higher powers dissociated from his strictly poetic props.

This anonymous poet is not the only *letrado* to address *preguntas* on theological subjects to Villasandino. Fray Diego de Valencia, as we have seen, challenges him on the subject of fate and free will. Likewise, Fray Pedro de Colunga, a Dominican, directs a couple of verses to him. These are, like the questions of the *bachiller,* clearly related to the theological pretensions of poetry. One of the pieces is also a riddle. Fray Pedro asks Villasandino to explain a vision which was once sent to a grave matron: she dreams that she has given birth to a dog with a lighted candle in its mouth. In answer the poet identifies the dog as St. Dominic:

> Aquesta grant dueña de suso nonbrada
> A Santo Domingo parió syn infynta,
> Segunt que un doctor lo pone é lo pinta
> Aquella vysyon le fue apropyada,
> Commo por perro la grey es guardada
> E por la candela que dél rreluzia
> Los muchos sermones que siempre fazia
> Demuestran grant gente por él alunbrada. [33]

The background of the riddle is the well known epithet applied to the Order of Preachers, *Domini canes*, dogs of the Lord. This pair of poems duplicates pretty much the situation of the first exchange with the *bachiller*: this is simply a test of the poet's ingenuity. Vastly more startling in every sense is the other of the two *preguntas*, in which Villasandino is asked to do nothing less than write a commentary on a chapter of the Apocalypse. The whole project is in the mind of the friar not likely to come to very spectacular results. Less sarcastic than the *bachiller*, Fray Pedro nevertheless says with some malice to Villasandino:

> Ruego vos que obrades el vestro decreto
> E me declaredes aquella vissyon &c. [34]

The irony lies in the fact that an admittedly unlearned poet like Villasandino would be unlikely to be very conversant with Gratian and the decretals. He says so roundly in his *respuesta*, in fact:

> ...en el latyn yo non me entremeto
> ¿Commo queredes que mi discreçion
> Bastase á faser tal declaraçion?

The commentary goes on in any event. The chapter in question, which Fray Pedro paraphrases in his *pregunta*, is Apoc. XII, in which John records his vision of the Woman in the heavens. Here is Colunga's version:

---

[33] CB 137.
[34] Fray Pedro's *pregunta* is CB 82; Villasandino's answer is, of course, CB 83.

> Dixo que viera muger en persona
> Vestida del sol, so sus pies la luna,
> E vyo en su cabeça una sobre fortuna
> De doze estrellas, preciosa corona:
> Clamava de parte en faz de Oryona,
> Que fijo varon avye de paryr
> E todas las gentes avye de regyr
> Con verga de fyerro, non sé sy es azcona.
>
> Des que fue nasçido el fijo varon,
> Luego á los çielos fue arrebatado,
> Delante el trono de Dios asentado
> Que non lo tragasse el cruel dragon:

Villasandino's exposition of these lines is lengthy, running to some eight stanzas. Heart of the matter is, of course, his identification of the woman — not an Amazon, but Mary, the Mother of God:

> Non fue esta muger la grant amazona
> Nin de las deessas fermosas alguna;
> Mas fue la que fyzo del pesebre cuna
> Para su fijuelo con voz de leona,
> Segunt que Isayas profeta rrazona,
> Que en una Virgen avie de venir
> El Fijo de Dios por nos redemir
> Por su santa sangre de linpia corona.

There follow some more lines on the prophecies, and a passage ponderating the beauties and excellencies of Mary:

> Aun que juntasen millares d'arvejas
> Con que contasen çien mill escrivanos,
> Non contaryan en muchos veranos
> Las sus fermosuras estrañas, sobejas,

A few lines further on, the poet spills over into anecdote:

> Asaz es propuesta su grant fermosura
> D'aquesta ques vasso de Dios é su copa,
> La qual fyso saya mejor que d'estopa
> Para su buen Fijo syn toda costura:

The stanza on the symbolism of the moon is interesting:

> La fermossa luna asy inclinada
> So los pies d'aquesta Señora gentyl,

> Será la Iglesia muy rryca é sotyl
> De muchas virtudes guarnida é dotada:
> La su color blanca é aun colorada
> Es que nos muestra caridat é amor,
> Pues dentro en el calis está el Redemtor
> Despues que la ostia es ya consagrada.

The rod of iron is explained as follows:

> La verga de fyerro será el grant temor,
> El dia del juyzio que á todos desmaya,
> Que non syento omme que en tierra non caya
> Temiendo sentençia de grant Redentor;
> Pues para que bivamos syn todo rrencor
> Syguamos las obras de los esleydos,
> Santos confesores de Dios escogidos,
> E asy biviremos en glorya é dulçor.

All of these fragments give us a fair idea of what is involved here. Needless to say, all of this is leagues away from learned commentary, and has only the most shadowy connection with what is in some of the standard expositions of the text.[35] A great deal of the poem is original with the poet, the interpretation of the rod of iron, for example, or the comparison of the moon to the chalice filled with the sacred Species. The whole *respuesta*, in fact, reduces the ambitious task of commenting the Apocalypse to an essay of pure poetic invention, compounded, like Villasandino's other devout pieces, out of topics of popular piety, anecdote and decorative detail. The importance of this must not escape

---

[35] For example, the interpretation of the "moon" seems to be completely original with Villasandino. According to Cassiodorus (*Patrologia Latina*, XXXV, 2417), Berengaudus (*Patrologia Latina*, XVII, 765), Bruno of Asti (*Patrologia Latina*, CLXV, 667) and Richard of St. Victor (*Patrologia Latina*, CXCVI, 798-799) the moon symbolizes the world, simply; for Anselm of Laon, it symbolizes worldly support of the Church, for Albert the Great (*Opera*, XXXVIII, 649) worldly desires, &c. It is to be noted that the Church is most commonly thought to be symbolized by the Woman herself, and that, in turn, she is less commonly thought to symbolize Mary. Joachim of Flora's *Expositio in Apocalypsim* treats Chapter XII in terms quite different from either those described above or those used or invented by Villasandino. It should be added that some of the Fathers use the moon as a symbol of the Church [G. Bauer, *Sternkunde und Sterndeutung der Deutscher in 9-14 Jahrhundert* (Berlin, 1937), p. 159], but in no case is this equivalence connected with Apoc. XII.

us. Commentaries on the Bible figure large in the reading of learned churchmen. Devout poetry of the sort Villasandino writes, here and elsewhere, is exceedingly common. But this precise combination, Biblical commentary done in the style of a late-Gothic Marian poem, I think it is safe to say is very uncommon. This poem is, then, like Lando's fragment on the Trinity, precisely a "poetic" treatment of a grave subject, made to order to prove the poet's ability to bring such a thing off. What is more, the whole exchange brings to light most dramatically the Spiritual background of the poetry-grace idea and the versified theology which grows out of it. We have here the spectacle of a layman, utterly without theological culture, commenting nevertheless on an obscure, exceedingly difficult passage in Holy Scripture. The anomaly seems less if we recall that the Spirituals made much of the ability of an inspired few to explain the mysteries of Scripture, taught, not by eminent doctors, not by authorities, but directly, by the Holy Ghost. [36] If we add to this the fact that the Apocalypse was a favorite text of the Spirituals, that all their supposed prophecies sprang ultimately from interpretations of this Book, whose dark wonders they were fond of expounding, the sense of this poetic dialog becomes clearer. [37]

We may now begin to summarize our findings concerning poetic grace. This special charisma of poets is at once a spiritual gift and a poetic excellence. On the spiritual side, we may observe

---

[36] For radical Franciscan illuminism see once again E. Benz, *Ecclesia Spiritualis* (Stuttgart, 1934), pp. 276ff. Ubertino di Casale teaches that Francis was the founder of a contemplative order to which would be given the spiritual understanding of Scripture [*Lignum vitae, Chap. III*, cited in D. Douie, *The Nature and Effect of the Heresy of the Fraticelli* (Manchester, 1932), p. 138]. Arnau of Villanova holds likewise that the faithful may rightly understand Scripture without theological formation [*Obres catalanes* (Barcelona, 1947), I, 141-166]. Manselli (*op. cit.*, p. 43) cites what he considers to be a typical case of a beguin whose spiritual and theological reading seems to have been limited largely to the Bible.

[37] Joachim of Flora, whose ideas form the very backbone of the Spiritual ideology (Pou y Martí, *op. cit.*, Chap. I, pp. 9-31) wrote an important commentary on the Apocalypse. Peter John Olivi's *Lectura in apocalypsim* [see R. Manselli, *La "Lectura in apocalypsim" di Pietro di Giovanni Olivi* (Rome, 1955)] enjoyed huge currency and prestige among Spirituals [*passim* in R. Manselli, *Spirituali e beghini in Provenza* (Rome, 1959).] It is evident in general that a great deal of prophesying by Spirituals is grounded, directly or otherwise, on the visions of John on Patmos.

that the gift is a "grace" in a rather narrow sense: it is a special light which enables certain persons to search out mysteries of all sorts, but eminently divine mysteries, the secrets of God. In its inner make-up the grace is apparently little more than a flash of intelligence, a stroke of wit, much the sort of light which enables us to solve strictly mundane mysteries. But it is precisely this quickness which is most useful to poets in the pursuit of their intricate and subtle craft. So it is that the "grace" is also an ornament in the poet, and is identical with wit — a quality poets are supposed to possess anyway.

In its inner structure this is what poetic grace is. In its practical application, however, this poetic theory is nothing other than an apology for ignorance. We gather this from the fact that the poets who believe in poetic grace are vigorous opponents of erudition in all forms, be it Imperialesque literary learning or scholastic theology. For our poets, poetic grace replaces or supplants purely bookish culture, and does at a stroke what the latter attempts to do slowly and painfully. It is this aspect of our theory, incidentally, the fact that it is an apology for ignorance, that makes us sense its very considerable originality. Thus we see that the poets who subscribe to it all pretend to be *provenzalizantes,* yet they connect their "Provençal" culture with something genuine Provençal poets never dreamed of, for nowhere in the poetry or poetics of the Provençals do we find, explicitly or otherwise, a programmatic rejection of learning. The whole drift of the precept and practice of the Consistory of Toulouse and of its Aragonese copies, in fact, would be decisively against such a rejection. In the first place, the professional formation of a poet as conceived by one of these institutions, is nothing other than a vernacular imitation of a university arts course. The poet studies grammar, rhetoric and the rest — not in Latin, to be sure, but in Provençal. Thus, when Baena writes, referring to his knowledge of Provençal and of the liberal arts:

> Yo leí los limosines
> Sus cadençias logicales
> De las artes liberales &c. [38]

---

[38] M. Menéndez y Pelayo, *Antología de poetas líricos castellanos,* II, 219.

he is not referring to two separate things, and the passage is not, as Menéndez y Pelayo supposes, a proof of Baena's wide reading. The *Leys d'amor* confirm fully our sense that the Consistory is an institution favorable to learning. Many grave authorities are cited in it, Christians and pagans, both. The theological arguments included in the *Leys* borrow freely from Augustine, the Victorines and various scholastics.[39] Furthermore, as one reads later Provençal poetry, one is struck with the friendliness of the relations in effect between the poets and Scholastic learning and we also independently know that many of them were persons of considerable reading.[40] All in all, the traditions of later Provençal poetry, in southern France, in Catalonia, and in Valencia have every aspect of a learned vernacular culture, a copy of the larger and more venerable Latin culture — a modest copy, perhaps, but still rich in its resources.

We may see clearly in all this the originality of the poetry-grace idea. The fact is that its defenders have not only put into Provençal poetics what was not there; they have also seriously misread and misunderstood this poetics. For Provençal poets the composition of works filled with high doctrine was in effect a way of imitating a more solemn sort of activity: for his Castilian follower it was a way of holding this activity in contempt. The poet of Toulouse or of Barcelona drank less deeply at the springs of learning than did men versed in Latin and to imitate him, the poet of Castile refused to drink at all. This whole situation is in a way a paradigm of the very special genius of our *enriqueño* poets in general. Their originality is partly deliberate and partly accidental. Their boldness and independence of mind are unquestionable, but often as not, their most daring enterprises are grounded on misunderstandings. The sense in which this is true in their "theology" is, of course, stressed many times in these

---

[39] The proof of the existence of God, for example, is based on a passage in the *Confessions* of Augustine, Book X, in which the mind is made to pass from creatures to Creator.

[40] Scholastic terminology is much used in some of this verse. One author among many who is fond of employing these technical terms is Arnau March; his "philosophical" love songs on this ground bear a resemblance to those of his illustrious nephew, Auzias (see A. Pagès, *op. cit.*, pp. 19-49).

studies. And here we have an instance in which it is true in poetics as well. The theory of poetic grace, a curious amalgam of Spiritual theology and Provençal poetics, is in a way a brilliant idea, but its emergence would have been practically inconceivable if its inventors had really known and understood the later Provençal tradition.

CHAPTER III

ASTROLOGY IN THE *CANCIONERO DE BAENA*

In our last chapter we made it clear that the doctrine of poetic grace was the occasion of a sharp division among our poets: the friars, who seem to have all been university men — theologians, canonists, or at least "artists" [1] — showed hostility to the idea, whereas some of the layman-poets were its champions. We also suggested that there were other issues which divided the two groups. The chapter which follows is about one of the most important of these issues, astrology. The way that astrology defines itself as an issue is rather complicated: there is no question of there being complete approval of its principles on one side, and complete disapproval on the other. Rather, it is a dispute between two somewhat different views about the nature and scope of the science.

We must make no mistake about it. There are many passages in the poems of clerics in which the authors seem to say very unambiguously that stars influence events in the sublunary world. Thus Fray Diego de Valencia in his allegorical poem on the birth of the future King John II of Castile imagines each of the seven

---

[1] In the epigraph preceding CB 323 Fray Lope del Monte is described as "bachiller en theologia": the epigraph to CB 245 speaks of "el maestro fray Alfonso de la Monja"; Fray Diego de Valencia is called "maestro muy famoso en la santa Teologia" in the epigraph to CB 519. Villasandino addresses Fray Pedro de Colunga in CB 137 as follows:

> Ffylosofo fyrme é grant metafysico
> En todos los cuentos de la naturaleza,
> ·Fundado en artes de gran sotileza...

"planets" making offerings of their peculiar gifts to the new-born *Infante*: Saturn gives him wisdom and prudence, the Sun, intelligence, elegant speech, and so on.[2] Fray Lope del Monte in the exchange with Lando about poetry and Grace turns the tables on his lay opponent in a way that bears out also his belief in astral influences. Lando in the original *pregunta*, enforcing his merits before the friar, reads him his very favorable horoscope: Venus and Saturn will sharpen his intelligence:

> Tomando de vos commo de maestro,
> Frey Lope señor, fulgente poeta,
> Entiendo yo synple atar mi cabeça [cabestro]
> Al çielo muy claro de Venus planeta,
> E luego en proviso por via secreta
> Seré proveydo del alto Soturno, &c.

Fray Lope reads the same horoscope differently, and sees the same planets inducing in the poet a most rebellious and malicious temperament:

> Polido en trobar, mirad lo que fundo
> Por astrologia de vos bien amada,
> Que Venus beldat da lo segundo,
> Ençiende luxuria mas desordenada:
> Saturno influye maldat acabada,
> Da nos pestilençias de su condiçion, &c.

Thus Fray Lope uses astrological doctrine to humiliate his disputant.[3] Much the same thing happens in the answers by clerics to the anonymous astrological prophecy for the "Cardenal de España." This violent attack on the bishop of Osma provokes two clerical rejoinders, one by the same Fray Lope, the other by Fray Diego. They assail the anonymous prophet on several grounds, but particularly on the *badness* of his astrology. Both clerics, that is, abuse him not so much because he uses astrology as because he is inexpert in it. Their attacks, incidentally, are themselves full of astrological lore.[4]

---

[2] CB 227.

[3] The series consists of three poems, CB 272-CB 274. The first and third are by Lando, the other by Fray Lope del Monte.

[4] The anonymous prophecy is CB 115. CB 117 is the answer by Fray Lope del Monte, and CB 118 is the one by Fray Diego de Valencia.

On the question of astrology, the significant difference between the cleric-poets of this time and some of their lay contemporaries was not simply that one group accepted astrology while the other rejected it. It is rather the degree to which they felt that the movement of the stars influenced events in the sublunar world. Thus, some of the lay-poets tended to attribute more to the stars' influence than did the clerics. The latter, as we will see, wished to set limits not only to the extent of the stars' influence, but to the degree to which their movements could be interpreted to foretell events on earth. To my mind, what was really under attack was the art of *judicial astrology,* the supposed technique of reading the stars at a man's birth so as to foretell particular events in his life, or the success or failure of his several enterprises, or whether the various circumstances surrounding his life will be happy ones or not. Once again, we must make proper distinctions. Neither the friars nor anyone seems to have had any objection to the use of the horoscope to determine what sort of *temperament* its subject possessed. The examples we have cited make it clear that this sort of astral influence met with no great amount of clerical objection. We can see the reason for this tolerance, if we recall that in the mediaeval view of things, subrational beings on earth, the laws guiding them, their natural history, all these things are largely determined by the stars. Thus, the physical part of man is shaped entirely by the spheres' influence. Since a person's temperament is dependent on his physical make-up, there could be no serious objection to the study of horocopes to the end of discovering what the temperament might be like. But carry the study very much farther than the study of temperament and of its consequences, and you will find that objections begin to be made. To try to predict how a particular warrior will fare in a particular battle, for example, would seem rash and suspect to some of our clerics. [5]

---

[5] Bonattus, the Italian astrologer of the thirteenth century, paraphrases the opinions of his theologian opponents by saying that the necessary and the impossible can be predicted by astrology, but not the contingent: "it cannot predict, for example, that such and such a man shall begin to move, or that he shall write" [my own translation from a quotation in P. Duhem, *Le système du monde,* IV, 194, from the *De astronomia tractatus decem* (Basel, 1500), tract. I, pars I, cap. VI, col. 6]. The point of view outlined

FORTUNE AND ASTROLOGY

Unambiguous references to judicial astrology are, of course, very easy to find in the *Cancionero de Baena*: it is indeed hardly necessary to cite examples. The anonymous prophecy for the Cardinal is a perfectly adequate case in point. Fray Diego de Valencia's ironical advice to the *converso*, Nicolás de Valencia, urging him to study his astrological handbooks:

> Niculas, estudia é vee sotil mente
> Los almanaques del tiempo que anda,[6]

shows clearly the currency of this lore. There is one particular sort of reference to judicial astrology, however, that is not so immediately recognizable, that hides itself under a set of technical terms. Such are references to the more theoretical side of the art. Thus, many of the discussions that apear to be about rather remote philosophical questions turn out in reality to be on the validity of judicial astrology. An excellent example of this is found in the great amount of talk about Fortune found in the collection. It is a fact that among poets of his time Fortune is simply another name for the whole network of astral influences that surrounds men. The more "literary" associations of the word, the great tradition of Boethius, Alanus, Jehan de Meung — all of these things are not entirely unknown to the *enriqueños*, but if they are present at all in their verses, it is as something accessory, as a sort of fancy dress for a homely idea. How far indeed the idea of Fortune can get from the bookish archetype can be seen in the following verses by Villasandino:

---

in my text is substantially that of the author of the *Corbacho* (cf. Media parte, cap. 3, *El arcipreste de Talavera*, pp. 341-348). The Inquisitor Eymerich also exemplifies this moderate stand. In a polemic work against astrologers he admits that the stars influence animal and vegetable beings (hence the physical part of man), but insists on reserving an area for angelic and human free-will, exempt from this influence. Astrology, he says, is partly good, partly bad; this work is paraphrased in L. Thorndike, *A History of Magic and Experimental Science* (New York, 1934), III, 514. For Aquinas on this problem see *Summa contra Gentiles*, III, Chapters 82-93.

[6] CB 477.

> Grant espanto es la fortuna
> Que todas las cosas sobra;
> Muy maravillosa obra
> Es oscureçer la luna:
> Quien mal fado ha en la cuna
> Non le viene çoçobra;
> Bien obrando nunca cobra
> De veynte cossas la una.

The comparison of fate to predestination (à la Wyclif) follows:

> Pues paresçe ser baldia
> La obra del qués preçito,
> Quien lexos ande del fyto
> De mas trabaja é porfya;
> *Nichil* en arca vazia
> Es todo quanto repyto
> Por lengua nin por escryto,
> ¡Tal es la ventura mía!
>
> Como al predestynado
> Non le puede dañar cosa,
> Su obra ffea es fermossa,
> Ningunt mal non l' es contado;
> Asy al que es engendrado
> En costelaçion dañosa,
> Tengo opynion dubdossa
> Sy puede bevir pagado. [7]

The piece concludes with a request for money from King Henry. Here what is most notable in this passage is — aside from the association of Fortune with the stars — the fact that Fortune is not seen here as something *mutable,* but as exactly the opposite: Fortune plays the part of a constant fatality, relentlessly pursuing her enemies, always at the side of her friends. It is further remarkable that Villasandino is not the least bit ironical about his account: there is no contrast stated or implied between his view

---

[7] CB 58. The doctrine of predestination here enunciated is very much like that expressed in the famous Calavera *pregunta* to Ayala, CB 517. Some feel that this doctrine is of Wyclifite origin [cf. M. Márquez Villanueva's introduction to Hernando de Talavera, *La católica impugnación* (Barcelona, 1961), p. 40]. I hope some day to complete a detailed study of Wyclifism in the *Baena* collection.

and the more "common" one, that Fortune is changeable. In this respect he is unlike his contemporary, Ruy Páez de Ribera, who opens his complaint to Poverty by attempting to correct the topic:

> Dizen los sabios: "Fortuna es mudable,"
> E non me paresçe que deve seer tal,
> ...Nunca mudança faze la fortuna,
> Ca sienpre en el pobre la veo seer una
> Fasta destruyr el bien prinçipal. [8]

Unlike Ribera, Villasandino is not modifying a topic, shaping it to his own purposes. Strictly speaking, he is making use of a second topic. "Fortune" is simply a technical term in judicial astrology which means "the whole complex of astral influence." Thus, one of the most popular handbooks of judicial astrology in the Middle Ages, the *Liber astronomicus* of Bonattus (who appears in the circle of the soothsayers in the *Inferno*), a work more "practical" than literary, opposes the idea of Fortune to that of Providence:

> "I would have you know that Fortune rules in everything, although some fools among those wearing the tunic [the friars, that is] say that Fortune does not exist, but only what God wills. But the wiser of them dissent from this in secret." &c. [9]

The author here is simply making an apology for his trade: these words have little transcendence otherwise. The Valencian poet, Jacme March, also uses the term Fortune to refer to the whole of astral influence. For him the rational soul of man is exempt from Fortune, that is, from starry fate:

> Quant heu cussir en los fets mundanals
> Totes las gents vey regir par Fortuna
> Segons lo cors del sol e de la luna
> Les planetas fan obres divinals
> Ffassen lor prou o lur dan a vegades
> Asi que'l mon es pertit per tornades.
> Mas Deu no vol l'arma sia sotmesa

---

[8] CB 289.
[9] Quoted in Thorndike, *op. cit.*, II, 830.

> Fforcivilment aytal astre seguir
> Ans la raho pot o deu ben regir
> Lo cors don han entre si gran conpresa.

In the case of March's ideas, God is entirely in command of the world-order:

> Deus es cuy es tota virtuts compresa
> E's ha format los cels e'ls fa vogir
> Pot si li play astre mal convertir
> E tot affan tornar en gran bonesa.

The moral March draws from all this is that men should pursue activities in which they are less subject to the stars' influence: valor, virtue, friendship, and the love of God. Incidentally, this whole brief work from which we have been quoting goes by the title of *Coblas de Fortuna,* as if to convince us even further that March gave the name Fortune to the collective effect of the stars' power on man. [10]

It should be clear, then, that the word Fortune in the Middle Ages can at times have an astrological connotation, and that its more literary connotations can accordingly be forgotten in these cases. Moreover, it is to be noted that when the more literary Fortune does occur in the works of some of the *enriqueño* poets, it is fully identified with the astrological one. A good instance of this is to be found in the poem attributed by Baena to Lando, written "quando echaron de la corte del Rrey á Ynes de Torres su pryma." The territory covered by the poet is largely pretty familiar: no estate in this world is certain, and those who rise highest are the ones most likely to fall:

> Algunos que suben corryendo fortuna
> A grandes altezas en termino breve,
> De aquestos atales non veo delyeve
> Quien biva su tienpo en firme tribuna:
> Antes por çierto, syn dubda ninguna,
> Tan beloçemente se dexan caer,
> Que non es bastante de los sostener
> Estelo nin poste, pilar nin coluna.

---

[10] J. Pagès, *Les "Coblas", ou les poésies lyriques provenço-catalanes de Jacme, Pere et Arnau March,* p. 35.

> Que segunt qu' el mundo a de costunbre,
> El omme non puede grant tienpo durar
> En trono superno nin alto lugar,
> Nin de rriqueza en grant muchedumbre; &c.

The poem, however, begins in a somewhat different mood:

> Pues que fortuna sus rrayos inflama
> E buelve la rrueda del mundo mudable,
> Non es provechoso, nin es saludable
> Sobir en triunpho que syempre reclama; [11]

Two details in these verses make it clear that Lando's Fortune is astrological. The first is the fact that the "rueda," the wheel which Fortune moves, is nothing other than the world itself: this is a considerable enrichment of the topic of Fortune's wheel. As we shall see shortly, Fortune is often conceived by our poets as directing and moving the whole astral machine: Villasandino, as we have seen, speaks of "fortuna que todo el mundo sobra." It is obvious that this is what Lando has in mind. The other point is that the "rays" and "inflammation," here applied to Fortune, are technical terms in astrology which refer to certain aspects of the stars' influence. [12] Both expressions are common in our collection. Gonçalo Martínez de Medina begins a poem: "Por nuestros pecados Saturno se enflama"; [13] Lando himself, in a piece which contains a series of questions on astrology, asks, among other things:

> Deçid esso messmo los particulares
> Que consideredes aquesta opynion,

---

[11] CB 277. Nelson Eddy, "Dante and Fernán Manuel de Lando," HR, 1936, points out that this work is not always attributed to Lando (p. 134).

[12] An Old French translation of an astrological work of Abraham ben Ezra speaks of the "rais" and of the "arsons" of the planets [*The Beginning of Wisdom, an Astrological Treatise by Abraham ben Ezra,* The Johns Hopkins Studies in Romance Literature and Language, extra vol. XIV (Baltimore, 1939); "rai" can be found on 46b, 47c, 52d of the French text; "arson" on 38a, 43d, 44c, 46a]. "Quemante" is the term used in the alfonsí *Libro de las cruces* [see A. Sánchez Pérez, "El libro de las cruces," *Isis* (Bruges), XIV, 77-132, especially pp. 81-82, 91] to refer to certain configurations of the planets.

[13] CB 333.

> En qué tienpo fazen su inflamaçion
> Las duras planetas, Saturno é Mares, &c.[14]

Elsewhere in the Ynes de Torres piece the poet again indicates that Fortune somehow is connected with the stars. The poem continues from the point at which we left in our first quotation (the poet is speaking of the man who is of high estate or wealthy):

> Ca es costellado en la servidunbre
> De magna fortuna é sus mandamientos, &c.

Man is bound to the decrees of Fortune by his star.

DANTE AND ASTROLOGY

This fusion by Lando of Fortune astrological with Fortune literary, with its particular set of, say Boethian or Boccaccian topics, represents something sporadic and isolated. A more widespread phenomenon of this sort in the *Baena* collection is seen insofar as its poets connect the name of Dante and his lines on Fortune with astrology. The passage in question is in the seventh canto of the *Inferno*; Virgil, speaking of God, the Framer of the universe, says:

> ...agli splendor mondani
> Ordinò general ministra e duce,
> Che permutasse a tempo li ben vani
> Di gente in gente e d'uno in altro sangue,
> Oltre la difension de' senni umani:
> Per che una gente impera, e l'altre langue,
> Seguendo lo giudizio di costei,
> Che è occulto, come in erba l'angue.

Men may hurl complaints at Fortune, the poet says a few lines further on, but she enjoys the Beatific Vision in Heaven, and so hears none of this:

---

[14] CB 268.

> ...ella s'è beata e ciò non ode:
> Con l'altre prime creature lieta
> Volve sua spera, e beata si gode.

Imperial, of course, echoes this passage very directly, in his poem on the birth of the Infante, the future John II.[15] Fortune herself speaks, referring to her goods:

> "De unos en otros los buelvo é traspaso,
> De linage en linage, de gentes en gentes, &c.

This work is, of course, the model of the *dezir* on the same subject by Fray Diego de Valencia, above mentioned, and both poems follow the same general plan. The seven planets offer the Prince each her peculiar gifts. Their speeches are followed by that of Fortune, who states that all these favors are nothing at all unless she adds hers. She claims, in fact, that gifts are in any case also hers:

> Ca lo que alguno se da ó promete
> Non le aprovecha si dél só enojosa.
>
> "Ca puesto, señoras, que vos le dotedes
> Thesoros, poderes, onrras, señorios,
> Commo á este infante, vos bien lo sabedes,
> Que los tales bienes todos son mios.

It is naturally here in the poem that the lines come which echo Dante. Elsewhere in the speech, Fortune makes it clear that she is actually somehow in command of the planets and their doings:

> Vos, Luna, bolvedes las aguas é rryos,
> Vos, Sol, verde seco en los naturales:
> Todas vosotras mas los mundanales,
> Yo los rrebuelvo en caluras é frios.

Her place is in the highest sphere, as she tells us as she promises to be favorable to the Prince; she is still addressing the planets:

---

[15] CB 226.

En mi alta espera, en el mas exçelente
Colmo le pongo, de las graçias goze,
De las vestras é mias é las d'estas doze
Ançilas é signos en el asçendente."

The reference to the signs of the Zodiac should impress us still further how close the connection is between Fortune and the stars.

A number of things emerge as we study this passage. First, it is clear that Imperial's Fortune is the astrological Fortune we have spoken of. Second, it is obvious that he has certain particular notions about the relations of Fortune to the astral machine; she is somehow its director and mover. Both of these elements answer to a well-established tradition regarding the lines in Dante. Thus, of the eight currently available fourteenth century commentaries on the *Commedia*, five explicitly read astrology into this passage. [16] Of these one describes a world-scheme very much like that of Imperial. Boccaccio, commenting on *Inferno* VII, says that Fortune is:

> l'universal effetto de' vari movimenti de' cieli, li qual movimento si credono esser causati del nono cielo, e il movimento uniforme di quello esser causato dalla divina mente. [17]

Like Imperial, Boccaccio takes Fortune to be the coördinated effects of the influences of the several spheres, and he sees the direction of all this activity as coming from the ninth sphere. Naturally, I am not suggesting that every detail of this account is of Boccaccio's invention and that Imperial could only have gotten them from him. As Boccaccio himself suggests — "si credono..." — the opposite is probably the case: the cluster of ideas is most likely common property. What is significant is simply that such ideas seem to be consistently associated with the *Inferno* passage, wherever they may come from.

Dante's lines on Fortune exert their influence on another astrology-minded poet of this time, Fernán Manuel de Lando. He too,

---

[16] See V. Cioffari, *Fortune in Dante's Fourteenth Century Commentators* (Cambridge, Mass., 1944).

[17] G. Boccaccio, *Il commento alla Divina Commedia e gli altri scritti intorno a Dante* (Bari, 1918), II, 216.

like Imperial, combines specifically Dantesque elements with the notion of Fortune as understood by astrologers. This is in a work we have already mentioned,[18] an omnibus *pregunta* on all sorts of astrological questions. One of these is about the nature of Fortune, her dwelling place, how her impulses can be overcome by men. Most significant from our point of view, the poet asks what sort of vision she possesses: "Qué forma tiene su synple vysyon." The relations to Dante of this idea — that Fortune is a sort of angelic being which enjoys the presence of God in Heaven — is obvious. It should be emphasized that this idea is not a common one: it is likely that it is Dante's invention[19] and that its presence in another is a sure sign of Dantean influence. We might even conjecture that it was Imperial who transmitted it to his gifted follower. We must note, incidentally, that for Lando Dante is a source not of poetic commonplaces, but of *doctrine*. In the works of Castilian poets of this time we may discover that what *poetic* influence of Dante that we can find is limited to Imperial himself. The extent of Dante's influence on other poets as a teacher, as a source of doctrine, seems to us a question worth careful study. Generally, it might be safe to say that except for Imperial, Dante's influence in any form on Castilian poetry becomes a serious matter only with a later generation of authors, with Mena, with Santillana, with Pérez de Guzmán.

Did Dante himself mean the passage in *Inferno* VII to be read with astrology in mind? His use of the word "spera" suggests that he in some sense did. Although this question does not concern us directly, it is important for us to realize that at least one, and perhaps all, of the *enriqueño* poets thought that he did. Fray Diego de Valencia tells us his opinion that Dante was damned for his belief in astrology. This is in his own *dezir* on the birth of John, written in the form of a *respuesta* to the Imperial work.[20] It also is meant to be a corrective to it, and the one great issue which Fray Diego takes with Imperial is his excessive attach-

---

[18] CB 268.

[19] H. Patch in *The Goddess Fortuna* (Cambridge, Mass., 1927), identifies the idea of Fortune as an intelligence that enjoys the Beatific Vision as Dantesque (p. 21). Nowhere in this work is the whole notion connected with any writer prior to Dante.

[20] CB 227.

ment to astrology. It is in this conection obviously that the Franciscan wishes to place Dante not in Limbo, but in Hell:

> Aliger non vido por quanto fue çiego,
> Segunt provaria sus dichos tratando;
> En que fues al limbo esta cossa niego,
> Antes fue damnado en infierno pennando: &c.

Incidentally, it is clear from these lines that for Fray Diego, Dante is little more than a reputation: he cannot have known Dante first-hand. Imperial in the original piece refers to Dante's meeting with Homer and Virgil in his journey through Limbo, but Fray Diego reads him as saying that Dante was committed to Limbo permanently. The friar's lines make little sense if we assume that he really was acquainted with the passage in the *Inferno* which describes this meeting. One wonders if Fray Diego's ignorance is not symptomatic. If we consider that the Dante influence in the Baena collection is scarce anyway, and that in Lando it is not literary, but doctrinal, it seems likely that what there is of it is second-hand, perhaps transmitted by Imperial himself.

ASTROLOGY: NATURE AND ACCIDENT

The word fortune, then, is one of the terms the *Baena* poets use to refer to the influence of the stars. One might easily make a mistake in this matter: it is clear, however, that discussions ostensibly about Fortune often seem to turn out to be in fact about astrology. There are still other terms used by our poets in expressing their thoughts on this important subject. Certain of these are borrowed from Aristotelian physics. In a very few passages in the Baena collection the merits of astrology are weighed under the aspect of the question of whether certain events on earth, or the whole of Fortune, for that matter, occur by *nature* or by *accident*; put otherwise, the question is whether they occur by *necessity* or by accident. This is, in effect, simply a way of asking whether or not judicial astrology is valid: those that hold that the events are *natural* or *necessary* hold that it is valid, while those that call the events *accidental* hold that it is not. This is the sense of a line in a poem by Fray Diego to the generous and charitable Jew, Don Symuel Dios-ayuda.[21] The poet spends some lines discussing the position of the stars at Symuel's birth, and tentatively attributes his liberal temper to them. In any case, he continues:

> Sy fué por natura ó por açidentes,
> Sabed, don Symuel, en toda manera,
> Que sy mas seguides por esta carrera
> Que nunca fué tal en vuestros parientes.

The phrase "por natura ó por açidentes" is, of course, the decisive one and should be read in the light of the intellectual habits of the time. Fray Diego shows here, in fact, a minimum of sectarian malice: the alternative he means to present is whether his Jewish friend's generous disposition should be explained in accordance with the ideas of the philosophy- and astrology-minded Judaism of this time, or with those of Christian scholasticism, somewhat less friendly to astrology. In other words, one of the views is supposed to be that of Symuel, the Jew, and the other, that of Fray Diego, Master of Theology.

The opposition *natura-açidente* appears elsewhere in the Baena collection only in an exchange between Fray Diego de Valencia and Villasandino in which this opposition is the matter at hand.[22] Fray Diego strikes the first blow: knowing of the other poet's interest in astrology, he asks with malice aforethought:

> ...desid me por vuestra mesura,
> Ventura, fortuna, natura sy es.

Is nature the same thing as Fortune and chance? Villasandino answers in the affirmative:

> ...con la natura
> ...son neçessarias fortuna é ventura, &c.

He continues and concludes by tentatively excluding free-will from the scheme of universal determinism. Fray Diego's answer,

---
[21] CB 511.
[22] CB 473-476.

a refutation of this determinism, which we will examine in due time, uses the same language. He paraphrases Villasandino in language almost identical to his:

...son neçesarias fortuna é ventura,
Pues natura, señor, syn ellas non es.

The very content of these verses — the fact, that is, that they are about universal determinism, and, as we shall see, the manner of Fray Diego's refutation — makes it fairly obvious that astrology is the subject at hand. Actually, Fray Diego's formulation of Villasandino's views is closely akin to that of the astrological fatalism of the Arab philosophers. Avicenna, for example, speaks of chance as the product of a whole network of natural causes which includes the heavens, causes which proceed *necessarily* from the *necessity* of the divine Nature.[23] We need not wonder in the least how this sort of philosophical lore could have been available and intelligible to Villasandino. It is astrological literature, precisely, which perpetuates it. Many mediaeval astrological treatises make a great display of philosophical knowledge, and tend to repeat just this sort of doctrine. Albumassar, perhaps the most read of Arab astrologers, includes in one of his works a passage on necessity and contingency, whose content is scarcely different from Avicenna's teaching.[24] It is probably not irrelevant to add that philosophical fatalism of Arab type was very much alive in Spanish Judaism of the later Middle Ages.[25] Jewish astrology and astrologism of this time may well have contributed to the currency of philosophical terms in astrological jargon. A witness to this can be found in an Inquisition record which mentions astrology: its language is very similar to that of the *Baena* poets. It tells us that a certain rabbi bore witness before the Inquisition that Felipe

---

[23] Cf. Avicenna, *Metaphysics* (Venice, 1498), liber II, tract. X, cap. I, quoted in Duhem, *op. cit.*, IV, 494.

[24] Cf. Duhem, *op. cit.*, IV, 476.

[25] G. Vajda in "A propos de l'averroïsme juif", *Sefarad*, II, states that in discussing questions about Providence later mediaeval Jewish theology in Spain tended to follow Abraham ben Ezra rather than Maimonides (p. 6). That is to say, it became very much inclined towards astrologism.

de la Cavallería (one of the famous *converso* family from Aragon) asked him to perform

> çiertos judicios a la judayca para que le devinasse que el movimiento que fazian los çielos si era *accidental* o *sustancial*, e si venia de parte de Dios o *naturalmente*, y demandando si pariria su muger o no.[26]

THE VIEWS OF THE CLERICS

We are now able to see somewhat better the import of astrology as a theme in the works of the *enriqueños*. We know now that not only are those poems about astrology which speak about it openly, but also a few others: those that speak of Fortune in a certain way, and those which make use of certain philosophical terms. The latter two groups, using, as they do, peculiar technical terminology, inevitably tend to touch on the doctrinal side of astrology rather than the practical. Thus, as we turn to the poems in which astrology is attacked, we are now in a much better position to evaluate the content of some of the arguments.

Immediately, for example, we find the schoolmen-friars deliberately proposing what amounts to a view of Fortune in open competition with the astrologized views we have spoken of. Fray Diego de Valencia states matters very simply. In his piece on the birth of the Infante, he says in direct answer to Imperial, let us keep the idea of Fortune, if we wish, but let us sever somewhat its connection with the stars; he says of them:

> Pues cata, amigo, que tú non te enclaves,
> Que pongas fortuna del todo en ellas,
> Ca muchos gentiles perdieron las sillas
> Por ellas fiando, pues non las alabes.

The "ellas" refers to the stars. As we will see, Fray Diego in attempting to separate Fortune from astral influence is hinting

---

[26] F. Baer, *Die Juden in christliche Spanien* (Berlin, 1936), II, document 466. *El libro de las cruces* (A. Sánchez Pérez, *op. cit.*, p. 109) speaks of comets and meteors as "accidentes," that is, they are not *necessary* occurrences.

broadly at the friars' solution to the Fortune question. Fundamentally, what they had in mind was to redistribute the realm of Fortune, withdraw great segments of it from the regime of the stars, to place it under another sort of influence, that of *chance*. Rather than maintain that there are mysterious forces at work which determine the careers of men, these clerics with a scholastic background wish to open a large area of human life as a theater for the activity of chance. To her can be attributed many of the changes of fortune, passages from riches to poverty, from honor to dishonor, to which men are subject. Now, as we stated, the conclusion that this is really the friars' doctrine of Fortune is far from being an obvious one. Taken at face value, many of the things they have to say about it seem far removed from any discussion of the nature of chance. Indeed, some of the friars' utterances seem to connect Fortune with very different sorts of causation. We must, then, state our case clearly and completely, and search diligently in our texts for any sort of hidden assumption which lies behind their teaching.

Two of our friar poets connect Fortune and her apparent injustices with the secret judgments of God. Thus Fray Alfonso de la Monja, a Dominican from Seville, answers a classic "complaint to Fortune" by Imperial by maintaining that she is just, that it is our fallible human reason that judges her otherwise.[27] Our understanding, in fact, is at a perfect loss to explain her notions at all; these are the secrets of God:

> Sant Pablo apostol con quanto sabia,
> Non sopo otra cossa aqui declarar,
> El dedo en la boca pensó de cuydar
> *O altitudo Dey*, grant sabiduria,
> Son mucho *inconprehensibiliçia*
> Los tus ssecretos é la tu judiçia,
> Que entender ninguno non podria.

The Franciscan, Fray Lope del Monte, is of one mind with Fray Alfonso in every respect on this matter. He too holds that to scrutinize the apparent arbitrariness of Fortune is to probe too deeply into the hidden things of God. Rather than search out

---

[27] CB 246.

reasons for unhappy events, we should trust in God and believe in His goodness. When confronted by a perplexity of this sort:

> El rremedio deseo segunt un dotor,
> Es conosçer omme non poder alcançar
> Los tales juyzios que Dios quiere dar
> E creer simplemente, por escusar error,
> En Dios é por nos non ser preguntado
> Por qué un malo es todo alunbrado
> Nin por qué el ynoçente passa tal dolor. [28]

Fray Lope goes a good deal farther than Fray Alfonso, however, in justifying his stand by philosophic reasoning. We have been quoting from a *respuesta* addressed to Villasandino, attacking the claims of astrology. The first lines of the piece identify motions of Fortune with God's secret judgments, along the lines we have indicated. There follows a stanza in which the poet roundly denies that fate or the stars have any power over human fortunes or that future contingents can be foretold: nature, he says, had nothing to do with men's being rich or poor:

> Non tiene ventura nin creo que fados
> En esto atal [Fortune's dealings] ningunt poderio,
> Nin aun la natura, segunt cuydar mio,
> Non fiso ricos nin pobres menguados,
> Nin los estrologos fallan por sçiençia
> Por que en esto diessen su clara sentençia,
> Maguer que se muestren en ella fundados.

We recognize immediately, of course, the astrological overtones in the word *natura*: it means, among other things, the astral machine as a cause of things and events on earth. In the next few lines, the poet expands somewhat his argument about nature, Providence and Fortune:

> E segunt que dixe en otro ditado,
> Juysios escuros son que Dios da,
> E quien bien lo pensare ansi lo berá
> De cada un dia assas platicado;
> Ca segunt desides, justo padesçer,

---

[28] CB 347.

Veemos al malo alcançar poder:
¿Quien lo jusgaria por bien ordenado?

At this point we begin to see the drift of Fray Lope's thought. He is hostile to astrology fundamentally because belief in it brings into question the goodness of divine Providence. What he is saying is that we must not directly attribute ill fortune to any *secondary cause*, like, for example, the stars, or nature as a whole. His reasons for doing this are clear: secondary causes are ordained directly by God, and to blame human ills on them would ultimately amount to pushing responsibility for the ills onto Him. Nature as such works only for good, and so we make a mistake when we blame her for the accident of poverty. Or again, the rule of the vicious is disorder itself, and nature is orderly: how, then, can we attribute such civil disorder to nature? To attribute ills to nature leads us into a dilemma: either we must deny that the ills *are* ills, or we must deny that nature is good. To doubt the goodness of nature is to doubt the goodness of nature's Author.

For these reasons Fray Lope prefers to connect ill-fortune with God's secret judgments, rather than with the stars. At this point readers may wonder if the friar-poet has not completely defeated his purpose. To what end, we might ask, remove the blame for human ills from the stars, if we are asked to put it directly on God? Why absolve the stars to save God's honor, if it finally means dishonoring Him directly? Fray Lope is prepared for this turn in the argument, however. God does not directly *cause* ill-fortune. He only permits it. This is, of couse, the perennial view of the schoolmen in regard to evil in general.[29] We can be certain that this was what Fray Lope meant from the comparisons he makes. The example he gives of "los muy escuros secretos de Dios" is election and reprobation: how is it that the thief was saved and Judas damned? Here the issue is very clear. God *saves* the predestined: He merely abandons the reprobate. A man's salvation is at every turn God's doing, but damnation is a

---

[29] Aquinas, *Summa theologica*, qu. 49, art. 1, "Whether God is the cause of evil". Also cf. qu. 48, art. 1, "Since every being desires its own being and its own perfection, it must also be said that the being and the perfection are good." Translation as in *The Basic Works of St. Thomas Aquinas* (New York, 1945), pp. 474-476, p. 465, respectively.

withdrawal of divine activity. We can never know why God saves one man and abandons another, but neither can we blame Him because some are lost, although we can indeed praise Him for the saved. The point of the comparison, then, is to underline strongly the completely *negative* character of ill-fortune.[30]

Human ills, then, are not caused by the stars; neither are they caused by God. Are we to conclude that they are somehow uncaused? This question is by no means frivolous. To answer it, however, we must make a lengthy detour through the writings of other learned scholastics. Let us begin with Fray Diego de Valencia, who, as we have seen, is also fascinated with questions related to astrology. One *respuesta* of his, addressed like Fray Lope's to Villasandino, uses arguments to attack astrology similar to those of his brother in religion. This poem is, of course, one of the exchange we have mentioned before between the Franciscan and the poet from Illescas.[31] In it, we recall, Fray Diego initially asks Villasandino if Fortune is the same as Nature. The sense of the question is, of course, whether or not Fortune is astrally determined. As we know, Villasandino answers this question in the affirmative. In Fray Diego's rejoinder — the *respuesta* in question — he offers a triplet of closely related objections to the poet's stand. One of these appears to be an appeal to experience. If as much of the world's fabric were determined by the stars as the astrologers believe, then it is pointless for men to take counsel with others on their affairs:

> Es por demas que ninguno llame
> Que bien le conseje nin mal en secreto,

The reason he advances for this is virtually the same one Fray Lope urges against astrologers in general: nature — including the stars — works only for good; if fortune is nature's offspring, it too is always good, and so to provide against its "evils" is ridiculous, as such evils are nonexistent. Our last question continues:

> Pues vienen las cossas syn grant defeto,
> Ca los açidentes non son humanales.

---

[30] Perhaps the most read mediaeval text on Predestination is the Distinctions XL-XLI in the first book of the *Sentences* of Peter Lombard.
[31] CB 475.

The turns of Fortune are not "humanales," that is, they are determined by a starry agent, not a human one. This argument from the goodness of nature is the second of Fray Diego's group of three. He reiterates it in expanded form in the following octave, using a favorite *enriqueño* example of the injustices of Fortune, the noble by birth and temperament who do badly at court:

> Muchos fueron ricos de grandes parientes
> Que syguen con mengua curso de palaçio:
> Tomen todos estos plazer con espaçio,
> Pues son neçesarios tales açidentes.

Fortune's victims, Fray Diego says ironically, may take huge comfort in the fact that nature is the cause of their troubles (*necessity* and *nature*, we recall, are pretty much of a piece), and nature is without defect.

Fray Diego's other argument is the one which in the poem heads all the rest: it is probably the most fundamental one of the three. If the astrologers are right, then *chance* is no more a part of the world's make-up:

> Si son neçesarias áçedentes tales,
> El caso é fortuna aqui se atame:

Fray Diego's *immediate* interest in bringing up this argument is probably that if there is no indetermination in the sublunary world, no "give," so to speak, it is futile for men to provide against ill-fortune. However, in bringing up the subject of chance, Fray Diego has hit upon a basic point for all these discussions about Fortune. It is, for example, the missing element of Fray Lope's argument. Put the dialectic of the two Franciscans together, and this becomes clear. Fray Lope does not wish to attribute ill-fortune directly to God. We could hardly expect Fray Diego to differ from Fray Lope on this, and although the *converso* friar is silent on the matter in this particular poem, elsewhere he frames an ingenious argument absolving God from such responsibility. [32] Fray Lope does not wish either to attribute ill-fortune to nature.

---

[32] CB 479.

Here, of course, Fray Diego is in full and explicit agreement, for identical reasons. Finally, Fray Diego "proposes" a third possibility not mentioned by the other friar: clearly what is not due to God's direct activity, or to nature's, must be due to that of chance. And we may reasonably guess that this was what was in the back of Fray Lope's mind too.

Actually, this is far from being a rash conjecture. None of our friar-poets is independently framing original arguments on the Fortune question. All are drawing from the common arsenal of scholastic philosophy. Once we realize that they are assimilating Fortune to the idea of chance held by most of the mediaeval schoolmen, the sum of their arguments adds up to an orderly whole. For the philosophy of the Middle Ages chance, the *concursus causarum,* was not a cause or a nature at all. Chance was what came about without the intention of any agent. A man who sets out to dig a grave and finds buried treasure does so by chance. That is, it was not his intention to look for treasure, and it was not the intention of the man who buried it that the grave-digger should find it. We can conceive of chance in sub-human nature as well. An animal in search of food and a stone falling may both be fulfilling their natures, but if an animal is struck by a falling stone, neither *nature,* strictly speaking, is to blame. Such happenings as these are, in a sense, uncaused events. If, however, we were to try to find any sense at all in which these events were caused, it could only be to say that God permits them. The following argument makes this clear. A chance event is a crossing of two or more lines of causation. Thus the man who buried the treasure did so because he was miserly, and he was so because of his temperament, and so on. For his part the grave-digger did his job for the money, desired the money to buy food, desired *it* because he was hungry, and so on. At a critical moment these two lines of cause and effect cross to bring about the finding of treasure. Do these two lines of cause at any point seem themselves to have a common cause? Within the world-order they clearly do not. However, since all chains of causation ultimately lead back to God, in Him we can indeed find such a cause. So it is that His compliance in some form is required for the chance event to take place, since in the long run He is the Origin of both the causes which bring it about.³³ We can understand now why Fray Alfonso and Fray Lope traced misfortune to the secret judgments of God, why Fray Lope and Fray Diego refused to admit that any intermediate power was responsible and why, finally, Fray Diego attributed misfortune to chance. What seems fragmentary in the scattered verses of the three cleric-poets seems an orderly whole in the light of scholastic doctrine.

The line of argument about the nature of chance may impress us as being in all likelihood the virtuality behind the thoughts of our poets. The impression becomes stronger, as it were, if we realize that other writers of the same century, writing under similar circumstances, made the virtuality very explicit indeed. I mean that later in the fourteen-hundreds we may come on vernacular treatises written by clerics attacking astrology, doing so by assimilating Fortune to chance and developing fully the scholastic definition of the latter. Thus one of the little cluster of treatises of Fray Lope de Barrientos attacking various superstitions is given over to the Fortune problem,³⁴ and his approach is entirely the one we have indicated. It is most interesting to note that he blames poets in particular for perpetuating the false notions about Fortune he wishes to attack. One is led to wonder indeed whether the churchman, who was close to John II, might not actually have seen the *Cancionero de Baena,* perhaps known it well, and found there in great part the occasion of his displeasure, in works of Imperial or Lando, say. Another treatise of practically identical content to that of Fray Lope is the work on Fortune of the Augustinian, Fray Martín Alonso de Córdoba, author also, of an anti-Wyclif tract.³⁵ It should be obvious in all these works that we are dealing here with some sort of preachers' and apologists' common-

---

³³ The schoolmen's conception of chance came from Aristotle's *Physics,* 115; the relation of chance to divine causation is, of course, not present here. For St. Thomas on chance, see, for example, *Questiones disputatae de veritate,* qu. 5, art. 4, reply, objection 7, or the *Summa contra Gentiles,* III, chapter 74. For Scotus, see his *In physicam* in *Opera,* ed. Wadding, II, 572.

³⁴ Fray Lope de Barrientos, *Tratado de caso o fortuna,* in L. Getino, *Vida y obras de fray Lope de Barrientos* (Salamanca, 1927).

³⁵ *Compendio de fortuna,* discussed in A. Sánchez Fraile, *Un tratado del siglo XV sobre la predestinación, en castellano* (Salamanca, 1956), introduction.

place, current already in the time of Diego de Valencia and his contemporaries, but reflected in literature more fully in the middle and late years of the century.

This line of argument against astrology — assimilation of Fortune to chance, or to the obscure judgments of God — is certainly the most widespread such argument in the *Cancionero de Baena*. There is one other one, however, one that seems to be limited to Fray Diego de Valencia, who is perhaps the most subtle and intelligent of the doctrinal poets of our group. He gives utterance to this argument twice: once in his poem on the birth of the Infante, the other time in a *respuesta* to one Nicolás, perhaps the same Nicolás de Valencia with whom the Franciscan exchanges verses elsewhere.[36] The crucial passage in the former piece — a work aimed, as we recall, at Imperial's astrological views — is somewhat less obscure than its companion in the other. In it he seems to be speaking of a certain disproportion in the astral machine:

> Non han los planetas eguales tenores,
> Nin çierran natura egual con sus llaves,
> Ca unos son grandes é otros menores,
> E assy fazen curso á modo de naves.

He continues in lines we have quoted:

> Pues cata, amigo, que tú non te enclaves,
> Que pongas fortuna del todo en ellas, &c.

Fray Diego is echoing here a widely used objection to astrology, a scientific one, strictly speaking, one that has a curiously modern ring. Let us assume — as did nearly everyone in the Middle Ages — that the stars affect sublunary beings. But in order to be able to predict earthly events by the stars with any accuracy, we must suppose that some of them return at certain times to exactly the same configurations that they have been in before. For this to be possible there must be commensurability between the periods of each pair of the planets in question. In modern language we would say that the ratio between the periods must not be a surd,

---

[36] CB 477.

must be a rational fraction. Now, say our schoolmen, there is absolutely no proof that this is the case: we do not know, for example, whether the radii of any pair of the spheres are commensurable. And so it stands proved that connections between the motions of the spheres and events on earth cannot be discovered even though they exist. [37]

There is no difficulty involved in supposing that Fray Diego drew this argument from some scholastic source. Although it enjoyed its highest fortune in circles to which he was probably a stranger, it also appears in the thought of Duns Scotus, the works of whom were probably known to our poet. [38] It might be noted that Scotus makes much of the complexity of the relations between the spheres and things on earth, and so Fray Diego would have no special trouble in finding the crucial text.

A FRUSTRATED DEBATE ON ASTROLOGY?

As a final note on the positions taken by clerics and laymen on Fortune and the stars we return briefly to Lando. We have mentioned a *pregunta* [39] of his addressed to all and sundry which treats of just such matters, the nature of Fortune, a handful of technical questions in astrology, and so forth. It is significant that the poem is directed explicitly to *both* clerics and laymen:

> A todos los sabios poetas seglares
> E los rreligiosos de grant descriçion,
> Presento rrequesta é fago quistion
> Por quitar de mí algunos pesares: &c.

---

[37] P. Duhem, *Le système du monde*, VIII, 443-455, discusses this whole problem. Abraham ben Ezra's treatment is dealt with on pages 444-445, that of Henry Bate (Abraham's translator and commentator) on p. 446, that of Scotus on pp. 447-448. Oresme's views are explored on pp. 448-454, and those of Gerson on pp. 454-455. J. and T. Carreras y Artau, *Historia de la filosofía española: Filosofía cristiana de los siglos XIII al XV* (Madrid, 1939), II, 443, assert that nominalism made few inroads in Spain during this time, and so it is unlikely that Fray Diego could have gotten this doctrine from the all-important Oresme.

[38] Fray Diego was a schoolman, a "maestro en santa theologia" (epigraph before CB 473) and a Franciscan: it is therefore unlikely that Fray Diego would not have been acquainted with the thought of the official theologian of his order.

[39] CB 268.

The point of this is that at least two of the questions Lando puts to his readers are real bones of contention, and would in all likelihood be answered differently, depending on the estate — clerical or lay — of the correspondent. Both questions are old friends: the first is about the *place* of Fortune:

> ...en quales lugares
> Está la fortuna...

We know full well by now that the lay poets would be likeliest to place her in a position of eminence, in the ninth sphere, or perhaps diffused somehow through all the spheres. The clerics, of course, would insist on keeping her on earth. The second question is about the music of the spheres:

> ...donde pronunçian los sanctos juglares
> Loores divinos de consolaçion, &c.

Here the point is that scholastic philosophy in general had little sympathy for the idea of the harmony of the spheres.[40] In particular it should be noted that the notion that the planets' periods are incommensurable to each other is especially destructive of the idea of celestial music. If the spheres do not move according to simple ratios, in what sense can we think of them as forming any sort of harmony? It will be recalled, incidentally, that when Fray Diego de Valencia speaks of this disproportion in the spheres, he uses a musical metaphor, as if to attack directly the idea of celestial harmony: "Non han los planetas *eguales tenores*."[41]

This omnibus *pregunta*, then, has every appearance of being an invitation to a grand debate. There would have followed a series of answers a little in the style of the group of poems provoked by Calavera's question on predestination, perhaps, yet unlike it in that the poets would have had to take sides in accordance with their estate. No *respuesta* to Lando's work has survived, alas! This is a huge pity. We would otherwise have been much better informed about the attitudes of this time towards astrology. This chapter, in fact, would have been much easier to write.

---

[40] For example, Leo Spitzer, "Classical and Christian Ideas of World Harmony: II," *Traditio*, III, 307-364, remarks on p. 314 on the hostility of St. Thomas to the idea of world-harmony.

[41] The underscorings are mine.

CHAPTER IV

THE RELIGIOUS IDEAS OF FERNÁN MANUEL DE LANDO

Doctrinal poetry — poetry about doctrine — makes up a large part of the collection known as the *Cancionero de Baena*. This is a manifest truth, one most reasonably repeated in all the manuals. The three preceding studies in this volume are, to an extent, witnesses to this fact. In a haphazard and unsystematic way we have tried in them to explore this odd poetic genre. In the present essay we mean to continue this investigation, but after a different fashion. Rather than pursue single themes — astrology, elements of Judaism, and the like — across a number of poets, we have chosen to study the configuration of doctrinal positions as they appear in a single poet, perhaps the most typical dogmatizer of the lot, Fernán Manuel de Lando. We are, in effect, going to attempt to draw the intellectual portrait of one of the most intelligent and, in a modest way, most original of the poets of his generation. In order to do this we will, of course, have to describe the setting for Lando's poetic activity, that is to say, we must somehow characterize the generation itself, paying particular attention to the place of doctrinal discussion within its production.

First of all, it should be made clear that Lando, Calavera and their contemporaries must not be thought of as a group of poet-thinkers who gravely exchange deeply considered views on philosophical and theological subjects. There is no philosophical Auzias March among them, no miniature Dante. With a few exceptions they are not interesting or penetrating thinkers at all. Their ideas, unusual or daring as they may be, hardly ever display any subtlety or complexity. Much less do we find in the poems themselves fine intellectual structures which serve as the basis for ambitious, strictly poetic conceptions. The thought is, in the main, undistinguished, and thought and poetry are rarely allies.

The fact is that to think of our poets as producers of ideas, as it were, is to distort seriously our notion of their peculiar genius, even of their excellence. The emphasis should lie elsewhere. The whole style of poetizing, the sociology of the group, supplies a key. As should be evident to every reader of the *Cancionero,* this generation of poets forms a closely knit group of persons, well known to each other and to their patrons. We can reconstruct a whole network of acquaintance by reading the poems: Lando and Villasandino are on writing terms, as is Baena with both; Calavera is known to a number of poets, as we have noted, and so forth. It is also fairly clear that most of these poems, whether or not they are addressed to particular people, are almost certainly meant to circulate within this small circle of poets and their courtly patrons. So it is, then, that the whole body of their work is like a large, uninhibited, many-sided conversation in verse. This poetry, which is so regimented with regard to versification and other externals, is therefore open and free as to subject-matter. The poetic convention allows, and even encourages manifestly "non-literary", autobiographical, anecdotal elements to enter the poem. Open nearly any of the *cancioneros* dating from later in the century and you will find the subject-matter of each poet considerably narrowed by all sorts of conventions, by commonplaces in whole systems. To an unsympathetic eye, perhaps, much of the subject - matter seems to be determined in advance. For the *Baena* poets this is conspicuously less true. Much of their subject-matter is manifestly *not* predictable. The poet's loss of his mule, the arrival at court of a famous preacher, the nobility of short standing of a friendly rival, matters such as these are grist for the mill of a Lando or a Villasandino. None of this springs from any sort of romantic urge towards self-revelation. The poetry is totally *ad hoc* and occasional because of the social pattern which it presupposes.

Now, it is in this light that we should study the verses on religious subjects. These are not primarily stock themes for lyric poetry: they are real opinions held by certain persons, poets or not. They are views known to the poets, or invented by them, simply as individuals alive at a certain time and place, and not particularly as men of letters, or even as people primarily interested in doctrine or ideas. Provençal literary conventions and Italian poetics notwithstanding, even in spite of the poetic-grace idea, our poets air their opinions in the same spirit and for the same reasons that they reveal other facts about themselves: the nature of their mode of versifying encourages complete candor.

The doctrinal poems themselves have several characteristics which mark them as revealing real opinions candidly expressed. In the first place, often in the course of these poems their authors allow themselves to intrude in their own work. Calavera, for instance, in his *pregunta* to Ayala on predestination [1] includes bits of autobiography: he has put questions on predestination to certain *letrados,* schoolmen, certain devout monks have attempted to assist him, and so forth. Lando, in his poem on St. Vincent Ferrer, [2] reveals certain personal attitudes. For example, he wishes to justify himself for praising a highly controversial figure:

> Non me quieran mal algunos señores,
> Letrados é sabios que son en Castilla,
> Nin ayan nin tengan á grand maravilla
> Por que yo desir d'él tan altos loores:
> Antes rrevoquen sus viles errores
> Los que contra él fueren rretratantes,
> Que muchos comigo estan concordantes,
> Teologos altos é grandes doctores.

Then too, non-literary intrusions of other sorts find their way into the doctrinal pieces. Thus even Gonçalo Martínez de Medina, one of the most rhetorical poets in *Baena,* allows some elements in his work which seem even utilitarian. One lengthy *dezir,* [3] largely on the "glorias mundanas d'este mundo," begins with "metaforas obscuras" about the Persons of the Trinity, a passage which, as we have seen, turns out to be simply a bit of anti-Jewish controversial matter. The work ends with a second polemical

---

[1] CB 517.
[2] CB 287.
[3] CB 337; cf. our references to this poem in the first study in this collection.

attack, this time perhaps against the "hard" doctrine of predestination, given utterance to by Calavera.

A further sign that the doctrinal poems are as candid as other verses in *Baena* is the fact that many of the problems treated are literally great questions of the day. The confrontation of Judaism and Christianity which we have spoken of is an excellent example. The currency of a predestination doctrine very much like that of Wyclif is a second, occasion that it is of a long series of *tenson*-like poems.[4] A still more striking testimony to the unrehearsed character of the opinions expressed is the fact which we return to many times in these studies: the poets, having little theology, are unsophisticated, even unskilled in dealing with their problems. They are often inconsistent. Sometimes they seem uninformed about rather elementary points of Christian doctrine. Lando, as we will see, is capable of describing the process of salvation without once mentioning the rôle of Grace. Calavera, in the same situation, apparently knows little of the doctrine of Original Sin.[5] We could put this matter in a more concrete way: the doctrinal poets in *Baena* are notoriously unlearned — the laymen among them, at any rate. Their boasts of ignorance are not vain. In the laymen's works we rarely find an argument drawn from reading in the famous schoolmen, for example, or from the Fathers. The rare bits of scholastic jargon they use should not deceive us. The university world of genera and species is totally unknown to them.

Bearing facts like these in mind, we are able to make saner judgments about Lando's poetry and thought. We may add, in the first place, that Lando belongs in every sense to the poetic world we have just described. He is indeed one of the group of restless independent spirits who are always at pains to inform us of their

---

[4] CB 517-CB 525. There is good evidence that the "hard" view of predestination enjoyed fortune in Spain outside the confines of *Baena*. Fray Martín Alonso de Córdoba's vernacular treatise on predestination, dating from much later in the century, is an attack on views practically identical to Calavera's [text in *Un tratado del siglo XV sobre la predestinación*, ed. with a study by A. Sánchez Fraile (Salamanca, 1956)].

[5] CB 525: "la nuestra alma linpia es criada" — Calavera places this statement in such a context as to suggest that our moral acts are the *only* factors determining our condemnation or salvation.

highly personal religious opinions. From a purely literary point of view, however, he is something more. He appears to be a member of a group bound by a common poetic practice. I mean the circle — which includes Baena, the compiler, Villasandino and others — who, copying Provençal fashion, fill up pages with endless *tenson* series, testing each other's poetic skill, disputing arbitrarily chosen subjects, submitting their contests to judges, and so on.[6] Broadly put, then, Lando is a *provenzalizante*. It is worth stating this clearly, since so many critics have attempted to make him something else, a member of that well known chimera, the Italianate-allegorical school. With all these things in mind, it might prove profitable to compare Lando to the most brilliant of the *provenzalizantes* in *Baena,* another restless spirit, Alvarez de Villasandino.

Lando, less facile in the Provençal mode than his confrère, but only half-converted to the style of Imperial's "learned" poetry, turns out to be in substantial agreement with Villasandino on the subjects of technique, erudition, inspiration and the rest. What is probably much more important, both poets seem deeply affected by radical Franciscan ideas. Both hold opinions that could be called illuminist, for example, and both boast of their powers as interpreters of Scripture, as we have seen. Then too, both seem also to be believers in judicial astrology. Absolutely fundamental to both is the belief they express that as poets they are in some way also called to be lay theologians, that unschooled as they are, they have a right to comment on Scripture, to probe deep mysteries of the Christian religion, directly inspired as they are by God.

In the thought of Villasandino, the less speculative, the less systematic, and — alas — the less intelligent of the two poets, the use of this prerogative is not hard to describe. He shows interest in several doctrinal areas. In the first place, his belief in astrology seems very thorough-going: at one point he hesitates to exempt

---

[6] The many poetic exchanges involving Juan Alfonso de Baena illustrate the sort of thing I am referring to (for example, the long series of poems CB 357-451). John G. Cummins has written an excellent article on this segment of the *Cancionero*: "Methods and Conventions in the 15th Century Poetic Debate," HR, 1963, pp. 307-323.

from astral determination even the free-will of man.[7] This astrologism seems to be allied to a very deep-seated fatalism which is highly vital and personal, and hardly intellectualized at all, witness his verses on his personal misfortunes.[8] A second doctrinal commitment of his, predestinarianism, perhaps also grows out of this fatalist mood. In one poem he draws a parallel between the state of an ill-starred person and one reprobate: both, he says, are totally helpless to better their condition.[9] Beyond these two points it is difficult to see much system. He is, for example, exceedingly capricious in his interpretations of the Bible, though not in such a way as to reveal any deep or consistent strain of thought.[10]

Here, then, is our term of comparison. Villasandino's attitudes towards religion are bold, haphazard, on the whole superficial. Those of Lando seem on the surface to have much in common with Villasandino's. His subjects of interest are not entirely the same, but there is in him some of his friend's randomness, lack of caution, much of his independence. On closer examination, however, we see that his doctrinal verses are animated by a spirit somewhat unlike Villasandino's. As we will discover later in our study, there is considerably more reflection in them, a much more consistent frame of mind, a deeper interest in the content of the doctrinal matter he discusses. Now it would be very easy to attribute this difference of outlook entirely to the unlikeness of the personalities of the two poets. There would be much justice in this: the mere difference in the degree of the intelligence of the two would itself explain a good deal here. There are, however, a series of very strange traits in Lando which are difficult to explain in purely personal terms. Thus we are forced to make reference

---

[7] CB 474.
[8] CB 58.
[9] CB 58.
[10] CB 87: the poet states that God created death because He repented of having created the human race:

>...fue la persona del Padre repissa
>Porque fyzo al mundo muger nin varon;

In Genesis God's repentance at creating the human race is recorded in connection with the Flood, not with the invention of death.

to a purely external circumstance of Lando's life, one which sets him decidedly apart from his colleague Villasandino. This is the fact of Lando's Jewish origin and background.[11]

Both poets show some sort of Spiritual influence, yet Lando's Jewish antecedents would lead us to expect this influence to take a very different and peculiar form in him. Now, there is a paradox in Lando. In his religious opinions — as I hope to show — there are large doses of Jewish matter, and yet, aside from his one excursion into polemic, there is not one Jewish source quoted by him, nor are there anywhere in his work full-fledged Jewish ideas or doctrine expressed. The Jewish strain in him is subterranean, and clothes itself entirely in conventionally Christian ideas and language. And it is precisely the radical Franciscan outlook which supplies him with some of these Christian externals. Thus a two-way relationship is established. We may say that his quasi-Judaism wears Spiritual dress, and we may also put it that his Spiritual outlook has a strongly Jewish coloring.

Lando's radical Franciscan or Spiritual bias shows itself almost exclusively, I believe, in his resolve to search the Scriptures, to examine the mysteries of Christianity, by *himself*, without authorities, without any other teacher than God. In this, incidentally, he is different from Villasandino, who shows Spiritual influence on several fronts. In Lando, however, there is a paradox in that this single strain of Spiritual matter works itself out in a way that makes his Jewish background visible. We may see the truth of this if we see how he goes about doing the searching. It is clear, for example, that he holds very special views concerning the *mysterious* element in Christianity, and concerning revelation. Underlying these views is a deep-seated tendency on his part to minimize the extent to which God intervenes directly in the affairs

---

[11] In the first study of this collection we have made reference to the Jewish background of Lando. It seems unlikely that Villasandino had ever been a Jew, active as he was as a courtly poet even in the reign of Henry the Second (CB 16, epigraph). Conversions to Christianity before the massacres of 1391 were not frequent. M. R. Lida de Malkiel speaks of Villasandino as an Old Christian [*La originalidad artistica de la 'Celestina'* (Buenos Aires, 1962), p. 367 n.]. It should be noted, however, that Américo Castro speaks of him as a *converso* [*Algunos aspectos del vivir hispánico* (Santiago de Chile, 1947), p. 21].

of this world. This too is a great help to us in locating the areas of Jewish influence in his thought. With this order of problem in mind, then, let us examine his ideas in two areas of doctrine which seem to have attracted his interest: Grace and predestination.

It is in every way striking, for example, that Lando often uses the word *graçia* in such a way as to minimize its super-naturalistic associations. Thus he sometimes uses the word as referring to a special gift of the poet.[12] Here, as we have seen, it seems to denote some sort of private revelation, to be sure, but a revelation which lies well within the order of nature. This "divine gift" consists in little more than a temporary flash of wit, a momentary quickness of intelligence, the sort that might be useful in the solving of riddles. It is no use in this case to say that Lando and the others in giving grace this special meaning are thinking only of the estate of poets. We know full well that Lando connects "poetic" grace very explicitly with other species of divine favor, God's illumination of the simple, for example. There is more involved here than merely poetics.

Grace is reduced to Nature by Lando in a vastly more dramatic form than this, however. In two crucial passages grace is treated by him not as an order superior to Nature, but as an effect of that thing which for Lando's contemporaries carried the name of Nature, that is, the astral machine.[13] One instance of this is fairly well known to us. We recall that in his dispute with Fray Lope del Monte he boasts of a horoscope favorable to poet-theologians, at the same time attributing his powers along this line directly to the grace of God.[14] We are left supposing that the grace and the influence of the spheres are for Lando one and the same thing. Even more explicit is the other passage, some lines from the poem about St. Vincent Ferrer, in which the poet is speaking of the saint's ability to bring about conversions. Here his words leave no doubt in the reader's mind that he thinks of grace as an influence of the stars:

---

[12] Cf. the second study of this collection.
[13] See the third study of this collection.
[14] CB 272, CB 274.

> Su firme planeta asy nos enclina
> Que luego en punto á Dios nos tornamos;
> Por ende, señores, syn dubda creamos
> Que bive alunbrado de graçya divina.[15]

The stars bring about *our* conversion: thus we know that the saint who preaches to us is illuminated by divine Grace.

These thoughts of Lando have, of course, only the remotest connection with what is usually meant by the word grace, and therefore comparison of the two ideas or schemes of thought may seem useless. One contrast must be made, however. If there is one note to the traditional idea of grace which is absolutely fundamental, it is that the bestowing of this gift must be referred directly to God, and not to any sort of secondary cause. Grace, for the schoolmen, is a gift that enables man to do what is beyond his nature, namely to share in the life of God and to see Him directly in Heaven. It is absurd, therefore, to suppose that grace can come immediately from any other source than God Himself.[16] Now, the importance of this fact for us is not simply that it might prove Lando is a conscious heretic. This is unlikely in any case: it is probable that he did not know enough theology to embrace heresy deliberately. Our purpose is rather to show that his philosophical or theological mentality did not readily accept the idea of God's *direct* intervention on the world-process. Our poet's use of the word *graçia* is really a test case. Whatever he meant by it the fact is that even with a term so heavily charged with supernaturalist associations he deliberately steered away from meanings which would seem to imply belief that God acts directly in the world.

We will see this fundamental skepticism appearing in other areas of Lando's thought. In one poem, however, he does speak momentarily of grace in a way which tempts us to believe that he had in mind some of the more normal meanings of the word. The work is the *dezir* on the fall from favor of Ynes de Torres,[17]

---

[15] CB 287.
[16] See, for example, in St. Thomas, the *Summa Theologica*, III, qu. 109-114, especially qu. 112, art. 1.
[17] CB 277.

the same poem, we recall, in whch Lando equates Fortune with the influence of the stars. Here is the first stanza:

> Pues que fortuna sus rrayos inflama
> E buelve la rrueda del mundo mudable,
> Non es provechoso, nin es saludable
> Sobir en triunpho que syempre reclama;
> Mas al que la graçia divina lo llama,
> Biva en el medio lugar de prudençia,
> Ca segunt que veemos por esperyençia
> De mas alto cae quien mas se encarama.

Here grace is connected with the moral life, and this is what gives the passage a more familiar sound than that of some of the others we have examined. We normally think of grace as helping men practice the virtues and gain Heaven by their free actions. It is to be noted, however, that *Heaven*, precisely, plays no part in this particular scheme. He tells us that grace inspires us to practice virtue, which in turn helps us to bypass the blows of Fortune, but nowhere does he mention the fact that virtue might have a further reward. The wages of virtue for him are paid in this life. Now it is quite true that Lando does not exclude the possibility that grace leads men to Heaven. However, the emphasis is clearly placed elsewhere. We need only guess at the background of his idea to see this. For example, the poet's turn of thought is obviously modeled on the completely naturalist quasi-Stoic proposition that good men are exempt from the buffets of Fortune. A further model is suggested by the importance of the stars within this poem. It is an old idea, one that kept its currency in mediaeval Judaism, that leading a good and holy life is the one way of eluding the whole network of astral determinations, that a good man is not subject to the stars' influence.[18] Just such

---

[18] Cf. Abraham ben Ezra, *The Beginning of Wisdom*, p. 152: "The beginning of wisdom is the fear of the Lord; that is the starting point, for when a man refrains from following his eyes and his heart in their tendency to satiate his concupiscence, then knowledge comes to rest within him; furthermore, the fear of the Lord protects him from the decrees of the heavenly bodies and from their sway as long as he lives." G. Vajda, "A propos de l'averroïsme juif," p. 6, makes it clear that in Jewish theology of the fourteenth century ideas about Providence and fate come rather from Abraham ben Ezra than from Maimonides.

a notion, in confused form, is the sort that might well have been lurking in the mind of a *converso* like Lando. And once again, the naturalism of the notion is obvious, as it is of so many mediaeval Jewish religious ideas. So it is that Lando is putting grace (whatever he may mean by the word) at the service of a purely natural end — bypassing fortune and fate — and, as we would gather from his presumed models, he keeps his idea of grace apparently well within a naturalist view of things.

In three different areas, then, we find the word *graçia* stripped of a good deal of its meaning. In a fourth area we find the word and the idea very conspicuous by their total absence. This area is predestination. It is true of Lando's idea of predestination as it is of his idea of grace that it reveals him very reluctant to admit the possibility that God acts directly in the world. The omission of the idea of grace from his scheme of predestination is an instance of this, obviously. In general, the idea of predestination is heavily loaded with supernaturalism in this sense, and so once again Lando's attempt to narrow the scope of this particular doctrine is very symptomatic of his religious outlook.

His thoughts on predestination are contained in the ingenious *respuesta* to the well known and all-important question on that subject addressed to Ayala. Now, the heart of Calavera's argument is the proposition that God is unjust in that He creates men He knows will die in a state of sin and hence will go to Hell. The poet is particularly disturbed by the fact that it is only God's grace, freely given, that keeps men out of Hell in the first place. Now, as we have hinted, Lando's solution to this dilemma is to reduce as much as possible the rôle of God in the economy of salvation. Fundamentally, for Lando, God is little more than a passive observer of the human scene. In no sense does He intervene in the course of men's lives, helping them to avoid sin, or even rescuing them from an original injustice, in which Lando does not seem to believe, as we have seen. Needless to say God's knowledge is conceived in such a way that free-will is left completely untouched. The truth is that nearly the only positive function left to God in Lando's doctrine of salvation is to judge, to reward and to punish. Lando sums up his beliefs in the form of an extended metaphor:

> Tal es el juysio de Dios glorioso
> Commo espejo claro é rresplandeçiente,
> Quier blanco, quier prieto, quier feo ó fermoso,
> Tal forma demuestra qual tien de presente,
> Maguer non sse muda su ser eçelente,
> Nin fas neçesario á omme engendrado:
> Segunt que nos falló en qual quier estado
> Assy su sentençia obra en la gente.
>
> Ca sy un omme de blanco vestido
> En algunt espejo sotil se mirare,
> Segunt essa guisa de que está guarnido
> Atal se verá desque se catare;
> Pero sy despues otros paños tomare
> De prieta ó jalde ó qual quier color,
> En esta fygura é mesmo tenor
> Asy lo verá quien bien lo oteare.
>
> Pues bien assy digo que la Deydat
> Acata á todos los ommes criados,
> Ca es un espejo de grant claridat
> En el qual todos estan fygurados;
> Maguer sus juysios nunca son mudados
> Segunt nuestras obras se andan trocando,
> Asy su setençia nos está judgando,
> Tan bien á los justos commo á los dañados.

Now, to reduce God's rôle in salvation to such a passive one is substantially the same thing as to deny the very existence of predestination. The heart of this doctrine, as we know, is the proposition that God in a positive action chooses those He is going to save even before they are created. [19] Elsewhere in the poem,

---

[19] This was the view of many of the great schoolmen (R. Garrigou-Lagrange, article "Prédestination," in the *Dictionnaire de théologie catholique*, XII, col. 2959). Certain mediaeval doctors, however, make less of the notion of positive predestination. It is striking to note that Fray Diego de Valencia's answer to Calavera, CB 519 (Fray Diego is a "Maestro... en la santa Teologia," as stated in the epigraph) makes predestination passive, as it were. It is also striking that of the three authorities he quotes, Peter Lombard, Alexander of Hales and Aquinas, two, Alexander and Thomas (the latter in the early *Commentary on the Sentences*, distinctions XL, XLI of Book I— his later views are different) make predestination passive also (for Alexander of Hales see his commentary on the same text in the Sentences, XL, XLI, in *Bibliotheca Franciscana scholastica medii aevi*, XII, pp. 400 ff.).

as we recall, Lando explicitly denies such election *ante praevisa merita* and declares himself in favor of the notion that salvation is *post praevisa merita*:

> E sy otros ante que fuesen naçidos
> Los quiso escoger é santificar,
> Fiso los Santos perfetos, conplidos [santos, perfetos,
> Por bienes que sopo que avian de obrar; &c.   conplidos]

Be it noted that here Lando retains some of the language associated with the idea of predestination — "los quiso escoger é santificar", for example — but the passage itself, and even more spectacularly the mirror metaphor and the poem as a whole, make it clear that these phrases are simply a manner of speaking, a way of keeping some of the externals and appearances of the doctrine while scuttling its real substance.

We have stated that rewarding and punishing for Lando are about the extent of God's activity with respect to the human scene. There is, however, one other way in which He is conceived as showing positive interest in the human race. He shows mercy to it. He does this in a rather limited way, to be sure, by seeing to it that the heavenly rewards men receive are in excess of their deserts, and that infernal punishments are less: "da chica pena é grant galardon." This merciful diposition of things is the result of the merits gained by Christ on the cross. Of Him Lando says:

> Mas quiso que oviesse muy grant demasya
> De santisfaçion é meresçimientos
> Para nos valer en el fuerte dia,
> Escuro, espantoso, de grandes tormentos;
> Que por nuestras menguas é fallesçimientos
> Cunpliese el misterio de su santidat, &c.

Christ's merits are applied to us in the hour of death to make up for the lack of our own. This is apparently the way the balance is tipped in our favor with respect to the after-life. This view of Christ's work, then, is one more instance of his theology. This is clear from the very fact that for Lando the effects of the Passion are felt by men at the end of their lives and apparently at no other time — Lando makes no provision for such, witness his omission of grace from the sphere of salvation. Thus we can see how consistent and thorough-going Lando is, in that virtually all his deviations from material orthodoxy show this single bias: at every turn he begrudges us the admission that God can act directly upon men and the world without a natural medium.

Now, we have said enough about Spanish Judaism of more or less philosophical type to be aware of the fact that it *too* betrays a reluctance to attribute events and situations in the sublunary world directly to God. Thus, it is not too extravagant to guess that Lando may have drawn this outlook from his Jewish heritage. The process of absorption may have been completely unconscious: considering his huge ignorance of theology, it is entirely possible he thought what he was doing was completely legitimate from the point of view of Christian orthodoxy. The Jewish pattern is there nonetheless. It is evident in things other than his skepticism. It may strike some readers as odd that Lando, being virtually a non-believer in grace and predestination, sees fit to use language that by itself would indicate the contrary. Why, indeed, does he use the word *graçia* to describe a natural phenomenon, and why does he speak of God as choosing those who in effect are going to save themselves? Were we convinced of the cynicism in religious matters of the Judeo-Christians, we would call this simply a dodge, a clumsy attempt to hide disbelief under a veil of words. Knowing that matters are not this simple, we may search for subtler explanations. The fact is that here again Lando is following a typical pattern of philosophical Judaism. It should not be totally unfamiliar to us. Jewish writers of the persuasion of Maimonides were, as we recall, constantly accomodating the language of revelation to their own naturalist picture of the universe. All kinds of events in the Bible, prophecy, for example, or miracles, were explained in terms of philosophy, with little if any appeal to mystery. Maimonides, in fact, devotes a chapter of the *Moreh* to show that the sacred authors ascribe to God directly things that are due to secondary causes. [20] This principle precisely could well account for much in Lando's practice. It would explain the odd ambiguity by which he attributes Vincent Ferrer's

---

[20] Maimonides, *The Guide for the Perplexed*, trans. M. Friedländer (New York, 1956), p. 249.

influence on others at once to the stars and to God, and by which he at one moment says that a man's salvation is God's doing and at another that it is in great part man's.

We could sum up the matters on the question of Jewish influence in Lando by stating that though there are no Jewish doctrines, or in a vaguer sense, Jewish ideas in Lando, Judaism of philosophical type supplied him with a general sort of method for thinking out religious problems. In effect, Lando turns onto the mysteries of the Christian religion a typically Jewish theological approach. Of course, this presence of Jewish influence does not in the least detract from Lando's considerable originality. It is, indeed, evidence of it. Moving as he did in ignorance of some of the most elementary principles of Christian divinity, it represented virtually a small stroke of genius to hit on such an orderly mode of procedure.

Lando, then, represents in some way a confluence of two dictinct currents, Jewish and ·Spiritual. His Spiritual outlook teaches him of his prerogative consistently in the direction of a dimly remembered Judaism. This is really the reason why in the long run his ideas bear little resemblance to those of his fellow philo-Spiritual, Villasandino. An Old Christian with little intellectual drive, Villasandino had no direction in which to carry his freedom, and the result is often little more than caprice. In Lando, however, everything is order and consistency, for he has ample material with which to fill up his Spiritual mold, that is, a typically Jewish attitude towards Providence and revelation.

The Department of Romance Studies Digital Arts and Collaboration Lab at the University of North Carolina at Chapel Hill is proud to support the digitization of the North Carolina Studies in the Romance Languages and Literatures series.

www.ingramcontent.com/pod-product-compliance
Lightning Source LLC
Chambersburg PA
CBHW020420230426
43663CB00007BA/1244